The trve principles of
pointed architecture
St George for England
St Edward for England

THE TRUE PRINCIPLES

OF

POINTED OR CHRISTIAN ARCHITECTURE:

SET FORTH IN

TWO LECTURES DELIVERED AT ST. MARIE'S, OSCOTT,

THE TRUE PRINCIPLES
OF
POINTED OR CHRISTIAN ARCHITECTURE:
SET FORTH IN
TWO LECTURES DELIVERED AT ST. MARIE'S, OSCOTT,

BY

A. WELBY PUGIN

ARCHITECT,
LATE PROFESSOR OF ECCLESIASTICAL ANTIQUITIES IN THAT COLLEGE.

KALPAZ

ISBN: 978-93-5128-859-6(HB)

First Published in 1895
Indian Reprint in 2017

Published by

Kalpaz Publications
C-30, Satyawati Nagar,
Delhi – 110052
E-mail: kalpaz@hotmail.com
Website: kalpazpublications.com
Ph.: +91-9212142040

Cataloging in Publication Data—DK
Courtesy: D.K. Agencies (P) Ltd. <docinfo@dkagencies.com>

Pugin, Augustus Welby Northmore, 1812-1852**, author.**
The true principles of pointed or Christian architecture : set forth in two lectures delivered at St. Marie's, Oscott, / by A. Welby Pugin.
pages cm
Reprint. Originally published: Edinburgh : John Grant, 1895.
ISBN 9789351288596

1. Architecture, Gothic. 2. Christian art and symbolism—Medieval, 500-1500. I. Title.

NA440.P84 2017 DDC 723.5 23

LIST OF PLATES.

FRONTISPIECE.

PLATE I.	Columns and Buttresses	*to face p.* 3
II.	Ancient and Modern Masonry	17
III.	Metal-Work	19
IV.	Ornamental Iron-Work	20
V.	Almery in a Reliquary Chamber	28
VI.	Ancient and Modern Roofs	30
VII.	Gable Ends—Ancient, &c.	34
VIII.	Ancient Wood-Work	34
IX.	General Prospect of St. Mary Magdalen College, Oxford	43

LIST OF VIGNETTES.

FLYING BUTTRESSES	Plate A,	fig. 1,	described page	4
Bulbous Covering or Steeple, in the debased style	,,	fig. 2	,,	8
Spiral Covering or Steeple, in the Christian style	,,	fig. 3	,,	8
Stone Tracery	,,	fig. 4	,,	18
New Sheffield Pattern for a modern Castellated Grate	Plate B,	fig. 1	,,	21
Patterns of Brumagem Gothic	,,	fig. 2	,,	22
Ancient Curtain Hangings	Plate C,	fig. 1	,,	25
Modern Upholstery	,,	fig. 2	,,	26
Ancient Pyx	,,	fig. 3	,,	28
Ceiling of an old house at Long Melford—Ceiling of an old house at Antwerp	Plate D,	fig. 1	,,	32
Ceiling of the Clopton Chauntry, Long Melford	,,	fig. 2	,,	33
Example of *ornamented construction* in an ancient timber house	Plate E		,,	33
Illustration of the extravagant style of Modern Gothic Furniture and Decoration	Plate F		,,	35
Street Elevation and Side Perspective	Plate G,	fig. 1	,,	38
Modern Church Towers	,,	figs. 2 & 3	,,	41
Christian Church	Plate H,	fig. 1	,,	42
Modern style of Greek Architecture	,,	fig. 2	,,	42
Old Collegiate Building	,,	fig. 3	,,	44
Misapplication of Italian, Swiss, and Hindoo Architecture	Plate I,	fig. 1	,,	47
Further examples of misapplied Architecture	,,	fig. 2	,,	48
Further examples	Plate K,	fig. 1	,,	48
Modern Castellated Mansion	,,	fig. 2	,,	49
Old English Mansion	,,	fig. 3	,,	50
Small Buttress—Large Buttress, subdivided in parts	Plate L,	fig. 1	,,	53
Illustration of the different effects of scale produced by large or small statues in the same space	,,	fig. 2	,,	54

LIST OF WOODCUTS.

(*Printed in the Letterpress.*)

	PAGE
A WOODEN Building the origin of Greek Temples	2
Section of a Pointed Church, with the Flying Buttresses decorated	5
Section of St. Paul's, London, a Church built in the revived Pagan style, with the Flying Buttresses concealed by a Screen	5
Groined Ceiling	6
Pendant	7
Boss	7
Bulbous Form of Steeple	7
Pinnacles	8
Section of the Dome of St. Paul's	8
Pinnacles	9
Pitch of Roofs	10
Square Piers supporting Arches	11
Splayed Piers supporting Arches	11
Arch Moulds	12
Examples of ancient Jamb Moulds	12
Examples of ancient Jamb Moulds	13
Modern Jamb Mould, weak and wiry	13
French Jamb Mould of the late styles, *extravagantly* hollowed	13
Form of an Arch	13
Caps at the transition from Jamb to Arch Mould	14
Ancient examples of Base Moulds and Weatherings	14
Feather-edged Joints	15
Base Moulds, Weatherings, &c.	15
Ancient Profiles of Corbel Moulds	15
Mouldings in Profile	16
Modern and Weak Corbel Moulds	16
Moulded String Courses	17
Joints of Stone Tracery	18
Well at Antwerp	20
Iron Tracery	20
Pattern of Modern Gothic Paper	23
Ancient Pattern for a Flock Paper	24
Pattern of Ancient Paving Tiles	24
Modern Fringe, composed of turned *pieces of wood*	25
Ancient Fringe, composed of threads	25
A Modern Valance of Fringe	26
Cast-iron Mullion	26
Stone Mullion	26
Ancient Woodwork	34
Modern Tomb in the revived Pagan style	40
Plan of a Greek Temple	40
Acute Pitch of Roof	41
Modern Collegiate Building	46
Sections of Pillars	53

PRINCIPLES

OF

POINTED OR CHRISTIAN ARCHITECTURE.

LECTURE I.

THE object of the present Lecture is to set forth and explain the true principles of Pointed or Christian Architecture, by the knowledge of which you may be enabled to test architectural excellence. The two great rules for design are these: 1*st, that there should be no features about a building which are not necessary for convenience, construction, or propriety;* 2*nd, that all ornament should consist of enrichment of the essential construction of the building.* The neglect of these two rules is the cause of all the bad architecture of the present time. Architectural features are continually tacked on buildings with which they have no connection, merely for the sake of what is termed effect; and ornaments are *actually constructed,* instead of forming the decoration of *construction,* to which in good taste they should be always subservient.

In pure architecture the smallest detail should *have a meaning or serve a purpose;* and even the construction itself *should vary with the material employed,* and the designs should be adapted to the material in which they are executed.

Strange as it may appear at first sight, it is in *pointed architecture alone that these great principles have been carried out;* and I shall be able to illustrate them from the vast cathedral to the simplest erection. Moreover, the architects of the middle ages were the first who *turned the natural properties of the various materials to their full account*, and made *their mechanism a vehicle for their art.*

We shall have therefore to consider ornament with reference to construction and convenience, and ornament with reference to architectural propriety. Construction must be subdivided and treated under three distinct heads,—stone, timber, and metal; brick might indeed be added, but as the principles of its construction are similar to those of stone, I shall not make any distinction; and as for plaster, when used for any other purpose than coating walls, it is a mere modern deception, and the trade is not worthy of a distinction.

To begin with stone. A pointed church is the masterpiece of masonry. It is essentially a stone building; its pillars, its arches, its vaults, its intricate intersections, its ramified tracery, are all peculiar to stone, and could not be consistently executed in any other material. Moreover, the ancient masons obtained great altitude and great extent with a surprising economy of wall and substance; the wonderful strength and solidity of their buildings are the result not of the *quantity or size of the stones* employed, but of the *art of their disposition.* To exhibit the great excellence of these constructions, it will be here necessary to draw a comparison between them and those of the far-famed classic shores of Greece. Grecian architecture is essentially *wooden* in its construction; it originated in wooden buildings, and never did its professors possess either sufficient imagination or skill to conceive any departure from the original type. Vitruvius shews that their buildings were formerly composed of trunks of trees, with lintels or brestsummers laid across the top, and rafters again resting on them. This is at once the most ancient and barbarous mode of building that can be imagined; it is heavy, and, as I before said, essentially wooden; but is it not extraordinary that when the Greeks commenced building in stone, the *properties of this material did*

A Wooden Building the origin of Greek Temples.

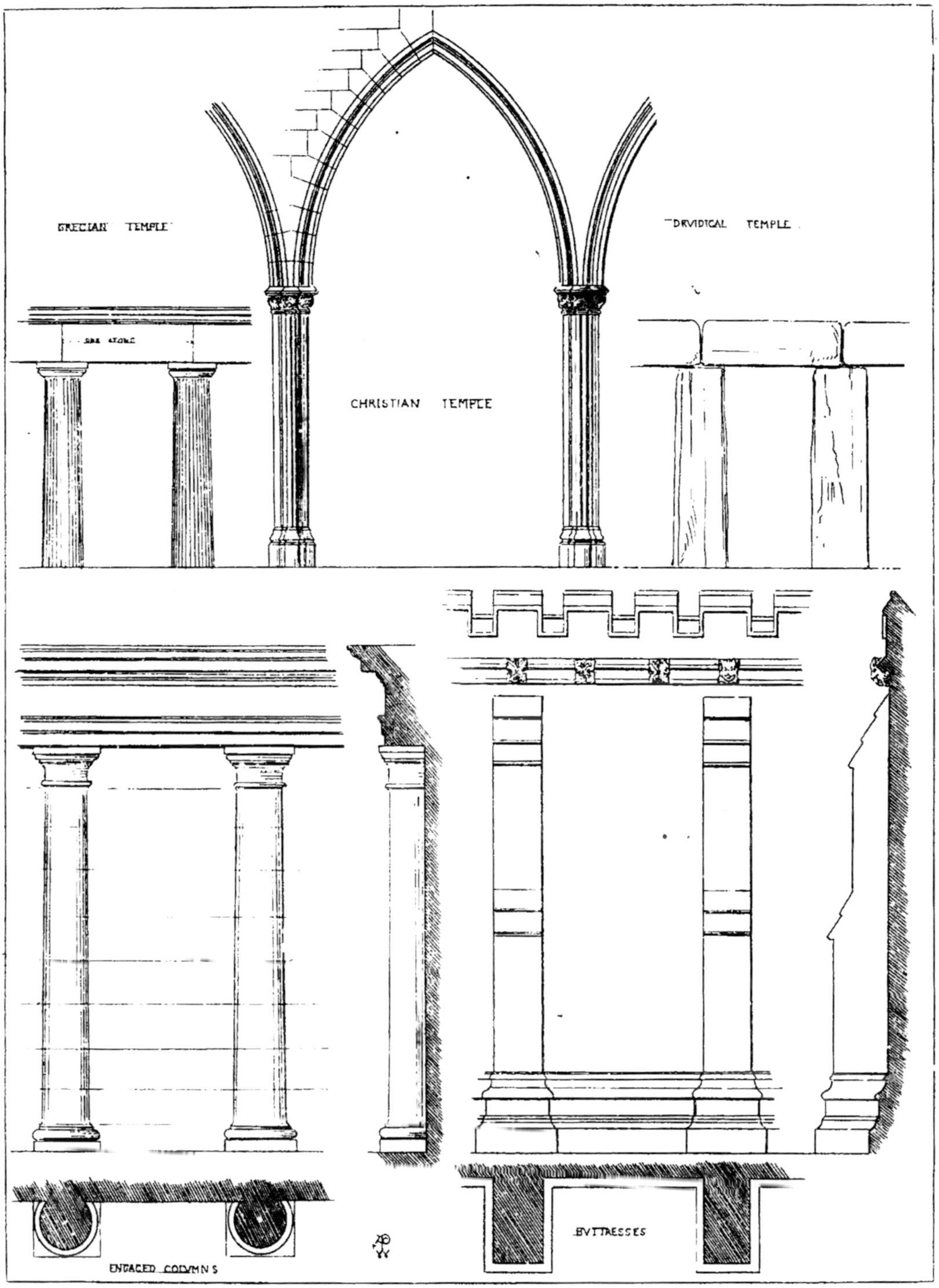
GRECIAN TEMPLE
ONE STONE
CHRISTIAN TEMPLE
DRUIDICAL TEMPLE
BUTTRESSES
ENGAGED COLUMNS

Plate 1

not suggest to them some different and improved mode of construction? Such, however, was not the case; they set up stone pillars as they had set up trunks of wood; they laid stone lintels as they had laid wood ones, *flat across;* they even made the construction appear still more similar to wood, by carving triglyphs, which are merely a representation of the beam ends. The finest temple of the Greeks is constructed on the *same principle* as a large wooden cabin. As illustrations of history they are extremely valuable; but as for their being held up as the standard of architectural excellence, and the types from which our present buildings are to be formed, it is a monstrous absurdity, which has originated in the blind admiration of modern times for every thing Pagan, to the prejudice and overthrow of Christian art and propriety.

The Greeks erected their columns like the uprights of Stonehenge, just so far apart that the blocks *they laid on them would not break by their own weight.* The Christian architects, on the contrary, during the *dark ages,* with stone scarcely larger than ordinary bricks, threw their lofty vaults from slender pillars across a vast intermediate space, and that at an amazing height, where they had every difficulty of lateral pressure to contend with. This leads me to speak of buttresses, a distinguishing feature of Pointed Architecture, and the first we shall consider in detail.—Plate I.

It heed hardly be remarked that buttresses are necessary supports to a lofty wall. A wall of three feet in thickness, with buttresses projecting three feet more at intervals, is much stronger than a wall of six feet thick without buttresses. A long unbroken mass of building without light and shade is monotonous and unsightly; it is evident, therefore, that both for strength and beauty, breaks or projections are necessary in architecture. We will now examine in which style, Christian or Pagan, these have been most successfully carried out. Pointed architecture does *not conceal her construction, but beautifies it:* classic architecture seeks to conceal instead of decorating it, and therefore has resorted to the use of engaged columns as breaks for strength and effect;—nothing can be worse. A column is an architectural member which should only be employed when a superincumbent weight is required to be sustained *without the obstruction of a solid wall;* but the moment a wall is built, the *necessity and propriety of columns cease,* and engaged columns always produce the effect of having once been detached, and the intermediate space blocked up afterwards.

A buttress in pointed architecture at once shews its purpose, and diminishes naturally as it rises and has less to resist. An engaged column, on the contrary, is overhung by a cornice. A buttress, by means of water tables, can be made to project such a distance as to produce a fine effect of light and shade. An engaged column can never project far on account of the cornice, and all the other members, necessarily according with the diameter of the column, would be increased beyond all proportion. I will now leave you to judge in which style the real intention of a buttress is best carried out.

I have yet to speak of flying buttresses (Pl. A, fig. 1), those bold arches, as their name implies, by which the lateral thrust of the nave groining is thrown over the aisles and transferred to the massive lower buttresses. Here again we see the true principles of Christian architecture, by the conversion of an essential support of the building into a light and elegant decoration. Who can stand among the airy arches of Amiens, Cologne, Chartres, Beauvais, or Westminster, and not be filled with admiration at the mechanical skill and beautiful combination of form which are united in their construction? But, say the modern critics, they are only props, and a bungling contrivance. Let us examine this. Are the revived Pagan buildings constructed with such superior skill as to dispense with these supports? By no means; the clumsy vaults of St. Paul's, London, mere coffered semi-arches, without ribs or intersections, *have their flying buttresses; but as this style of architecture does not admit of the great principle of decorating utility,* these buttresses, instead of being made *ornamental, are concealed by an enormous screen,* going entirely round *the building. So that in fact one half of the edifice is built to conceal the other.* Miserable expedient! worthy only of the debased style in which it has been resorted to.

Plate A

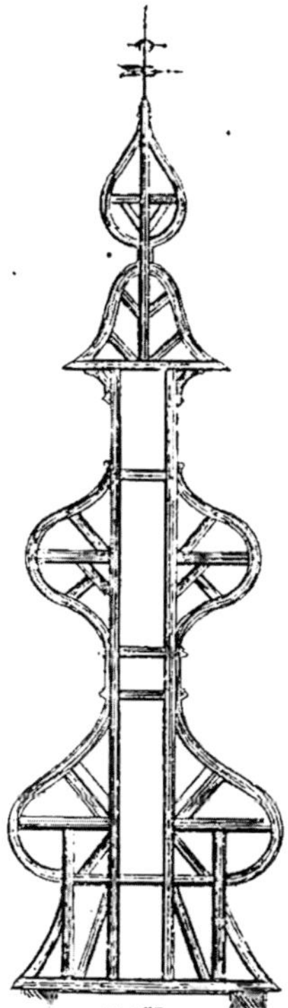

Fig II

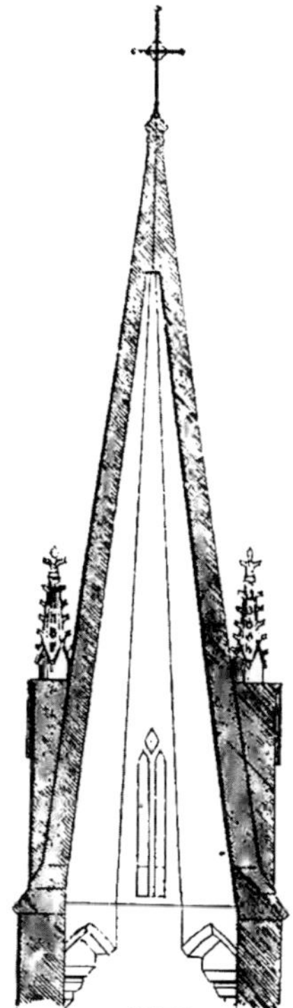

Fig III

Fig IV

Fig I

Section of a Pointed Church, with the Flying Buttresses decorated.

Section of St. Paul's, London, a Church built in the revived Pagan style, with the Flying Buttresses concealed by a Screen.

It is proper to remark that the cluster of pinnacles at A are not carried up for *mere ornament*, but, by their *weight*, to increase the resistance of the great pinnacle at the point of thrust.

We will now proceed, in the second place, to consider groining and vaulting, which are solely adapted to stone construction.

A groined ceiling is divided into compartments by means of ribs springing from caps or corbels, and uniting in bosses placed at the intersections; the spaces between the ribs are termed spandrils : the word boss signifies a spring of water, and has doubtless been applied to the key-stones of vaults, as the ribs seem to spring or separate from them.

Here again the great principle of decorating utility is to be observed. A stone ceiling is most essential in a large church, both for durability, security from fire,[1] and conveyance of sound. It is impossible to conceive stone ceilings better contrived than those of the ancient churches; they are at once light, substantial, beautiful, and lofty. 1st. They are light, because, their principal strength lying in the ribs, the intermediate spaces or spandrils are filled in with small light stones. 2nd. They are substantial, for all the stones being cut to a centre and forming portions of a curve, when united they are capable of resisting immense pressure, the keys or bosses wedging all together. 3rd. They are beautiful, for no ceiling can be conceived more graceful and elegant than a long perspective of lines and arches radiating from exquisitely carved centres. 4th. They are lofty, not only on account of the elevation at which they are placed, but that their construction permits the clerestory windows to be carried up level with the crown of the arch in the intermediate spaces.

In the groining of the later styles we find a great departure from the severe and consistent principles I have been describing. Henry the Seventh's Chapel at Westminster is justly considered one of the most wonderful examples of ingenious construction and elaborate fan groining in the world, but at the same time it exhibits the commencement of the bad taste, by *constructing the ornament instead of confining it to the enrichment of its construction.* I allude to the stone pendants of the ceiling, which are certainly extravagances. A key-stone is *necessary* for

[1] Within the last few years the roofs have been burnt off the cathedrals of Rouen, Chartres, and Bruges; and, owing to the strength of the stone vaulting, the interiors of these churches have scarcely been injured; while York Minster has twice been completely gutted within a short period through the want of a stone groining; and yet a mere wood and plaster ceiling has been again constructed!

the support of arched ribs; the older architects contented themselves with enriching it with foliage or figures, but those of the later styles allowed

Pendant.

Boss.

four or five feet of *unnecessary stone to hang down into the church*, and from it to branch other ribs upwards. This is at most an ingenious trick, and quite unworthy of the severity of Pointed or Christian architecture.[1]

---

[1] This is one among many other symptoms of decline apparent in the later works in the pointed style. The moment the *flat* or *four-centred arch* was introduced, the spirit of Christian architecture was on the wane. *Height* or the *vertical principle*, emblematical of the resurrection, is the very essence of Christian architecture. It was to attain greater elevation with a given width that the pointed arch was employed; and the four-centred arch does not possess equal advantage in this respect with the old semi; and although some of the later buildings, as King's College Chapel, Cambridge, still retain the principle of internal height, with the use of the depressed arch, yet who can avoid being struck with the inconsistency of running up walls to a prodigious elevation, and then, instead of *carrying out the principle, and springing a lofty groin*, losing a considerable increase of height by a flattened thrusting arched ceiling; the form of which is a sort of contradiction to the height at which it is commenced.

I do not make this observation by way of disparaging the merits of this stupendous building, but merely to show the early decay of the true principles of pointed architecture which may be traced even in that glorious pile.

We not unfrequently find the bulbous form employed in the Tudor period: this, which afterwards became the prevailing form of the Dresden and Flemish steeples, is of *the worst possible taste; and why?* Because *it is a form which does not result from any consistent mode of constructing a covering*, and, on the contrary, requires by its shape *to be constructed*, as will be seen by the annexed

In the third place, we will proceed to the use and intention of pinnacles and spiral terminations. I have little doubt that pinnacles are considered by the majority of persons as mere ornamental excrescences, introduced solely for picturesque effect. The very reverse of these is the case; and I shall be able to shew you that their introduction is warranted by the soundest principles of construction and design. They should be regarded as answering a double intention, both mystical and natural: their mystical intention is, like other vertical lines and terminations of Christian architecture, to represent an emblem of the Resurrection; their natural intention is that of an upper weathering, to throw off rain. The most useful covering for this purpose, and the one that would naturally suggest itself, is of the form represented in the annexed figure: only let this *essential form* be *decorated* with a finial and crockets, and we have at once a perfect

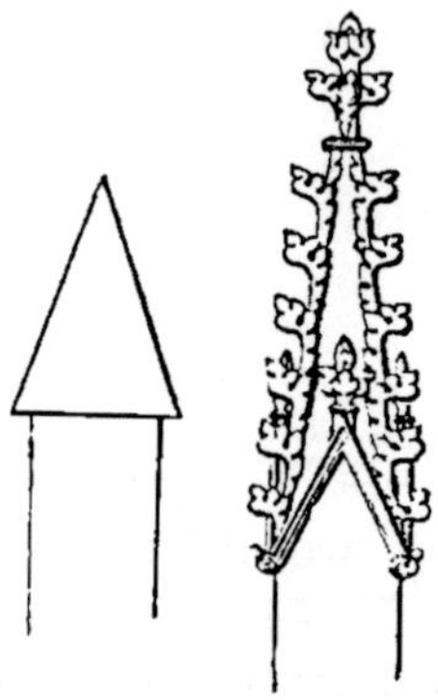

---

sketch; by the side of which I have placed a spire, the severe form and decoration of which are quite consistent with the true principles of rendering the necessary roof or covering of a tower elegant in appearance, without *departing* from *essential construction* for the sake of *ornament*. (Plate A, Fig. 2 & 3.)

One of the greatest defects of St. Paul's, London, is its fictitious dome. *The dome that is seen* is not *the dome of the church*, but a mere construction for effect. At St. Peter's the dome *is the actual covering of the building*, and is therefore constructed in that respect on the true principle; but, as will be perceived by the annexed section, the upper part of St. Paul's is mere imposing show, constructed at a vast expense without any legitimate reason.

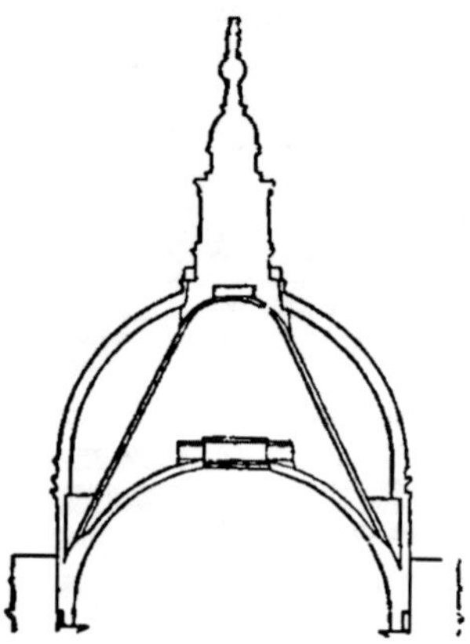

Section of the Dome of St. Paul's.

From the various symptoms of decline which I have shewn to have existed in the later pointed works, I feel convinced that Christian architecture had gone its length, and it must necessarily have destroyed itself by departing from its own principles in the pursuit of novelty, or it must have fallen back on its pure and ancient models. This is quite borne out by existing facts. Now that the pointed style is reviving, we cannot

pinnacle. Now the square piers of which these floriated tops form the terminations are all erected to answer a useful purpose; when they rise from the tops of wall buttresses, they serve as piers to strengthen the parapet, which would be exceedingly weak without some such support. Fig. S.

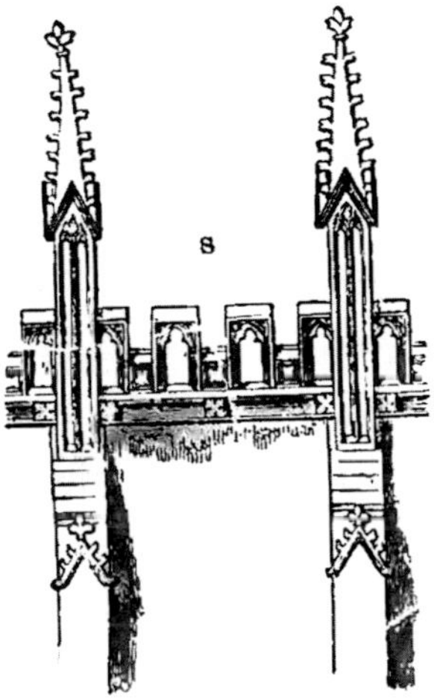

Their utility on the great piers which resist the flying buttresses has been already mentioned under the head of buttress. At the bases of great spires, the clusters of pinnacles are also placed to increase strength and resistance; in short, wherever pinnacles are introduced in pure pointed architecture, they will be found on examination to fulfil a useful end.

The same remarks will apply to the crocketed and floriated terminations of staircase and other turrets, which are in fact ornamented roofs; and I need hardly remark that turrets were not carried up without a legitimate reason.

Every tower built during the pure style of pointed architecture either was, or was intended to be, surmounted by a spire, which is the natural covering for a tower; a flat roof is both contrary to the spirit of the style, and it is also practically bad. There is no instance before the year 1400 of a church tower being erected without *the intention at least* of being covered

---

successfully suggest any thing new, but are obliged to return to the spirit of the ancient work.

Indeed, if we view pointed architecture in its true light as Christian art, as the faith itself *is perfect, so are the principles on which it is founded.* We may indeed improve in mechanical contrivances to expedite its execution, we may even increase its scale and grandeur; but we can *never successfully deviate one tittle from the spirit and principles* of pointed architecture. We must rest content to *follow*, not to *lead;* we may indeed widen the road which our Catholic forefathers formed, but we can never depart from their track without a certainty of failure being the result of our presumption.

or surmounted by a spire; and those towers antecedent to that period which we find without such terminations have either been left incomplete for want of funds, weakness in the sub-structure, or some casual impediment,—or the spires, which were often of timber covered with lead, have been pulled down for the sake of their material.[3] In fine, when towers were erected with flat embattled tops, *Christian architecture was on the decline*, and the omission of the ancient and appropriate termination was strong evidence of that fact. Towers surmounting gate-houses were never terminated by spires, for, being originally built for defence, the space at top was required for that purpose. This is the real reason why square-topped and embattled towers are said to be of a domestic character; so that even by persons unacquainted with the use and intentions of spires, they are associated with the idea of ecclesiastical architecture.

The pitch of roof in pointed architecture is another subject on which some useful observations may be made. It will be found, on examination, that the most beautiful pitch of a roof or gable end is an inclination sufficiently steep to throw off snow without giving the slate or lead

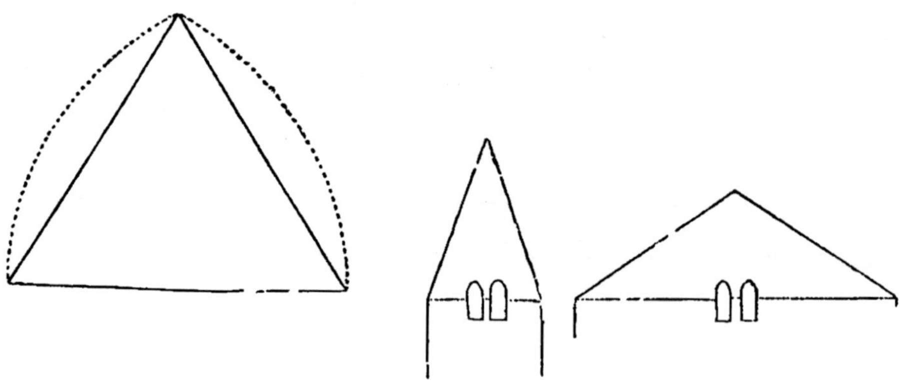

[3] The following glorious churches have been stripped of their spires since the views in Dugdale's Monasticon were taken:—Hereford Cathedral, Worcester Cathedral, Southwell Minster, Rochester Cathedral, Ely Cathedral, Ripon Minster, Finchal Abbey, and Lincoln Cathedral. It is to be remembered that these views were taken *above a century after the lead-stripping and spire-demolishing period commenced.*

covering *too perpendicular a strain*, which is formed by two sides on an equilateral triangle.

If this form be departed from, the gable appears either painfully acute or too widely spread. All really beautiful forms in architecture are based on the soundest principles of utility.

Practical men know that flat-pitched roofs, which are exceedingly ugly in appearance, are also but ill-calculated to resist the action of weather. In slated roofs especially, gusts of wind actually blow under and lift up the covering: when the pitch is increased to its proper elevation, the whole pressure of the wind is *lateral*, and forces the covering closer to the roof.

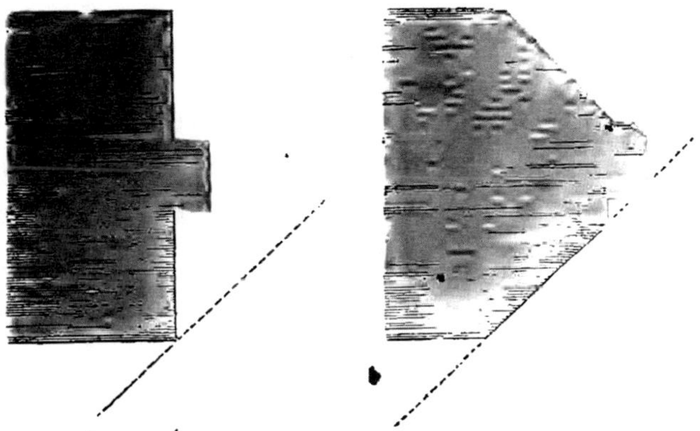

I come now to speak, in the fourth place, of mouldings, on the judicious form and disposition of which a very considerable part of the effect of the building depends. Mouldings are the enrichment of splays of doorways, windows, arches, and piers, of base and string-courses, of weatherings and copings, and they are introduced solely on the principle of decorating the useful.

I will first point out the necessity of these splays and weatherings, and then proceed to consider the form and application of mouldings to them.

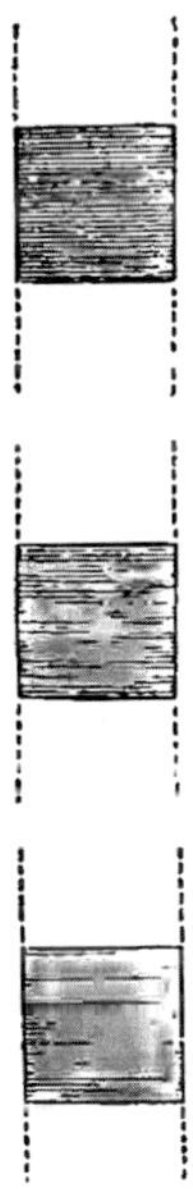

Square Piers supporting Arches.

Splayed Piers supporting Arches.

It will be readily seen that without a

splay a considerable portion of light would be excluded, and that this form of jamb is necessary to the use and intention of a window.

In a doorway the convenience of splayed sides must be evident for ordinary ingress and egress. This form of jamb is therefore necessary to the use and intention of a doorway.

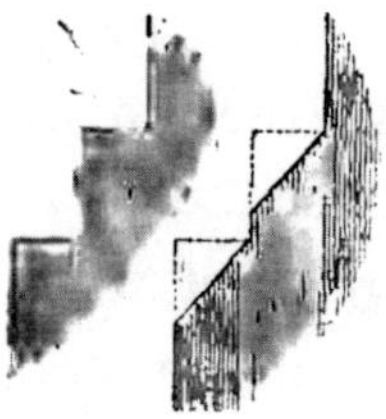

The advantage of piers splayed, or placed diagonally over square ones, both for elegance and convenience, must be evident to all; the arch mould over them is consequently splayed. This form of pier and arch mould is therefore necessary for both piers and arches.

Great increase of solidity and strength is gained by projections at the base of a building as sets-off; but were these projections left flat at top instead of being bevelled off, they would become lodgments for water.

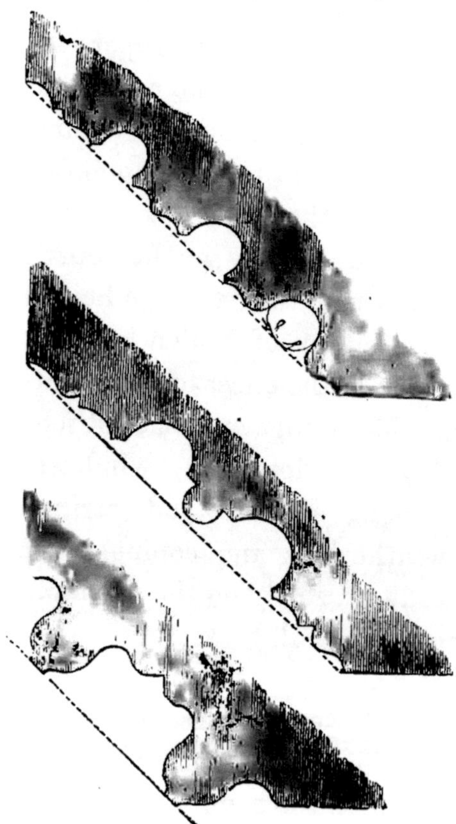

Examples of ancient Jamb Moulds.

The splayed or bevelled form is therefore necessary for base moulds. Strings and copings, the very intention of which is to throw off water, must be sloped for the same reason.

The use of the splayed form being now demonstrated, I will proceed to consider the mouldings used to enrich it. All mouldings should be designed on the principle of light, shadow, and half tint; and the section of a moulding should be of such a form as to produce various and pleasing gradations of light and shadow. Monotony should be carefully avoided, also all cutting shadows near the outer edge, which have a meagre effect. The original splayed form should never be lost sight of in the sinkings of the mould, which ought not to be so extravagantly deep as to produce both a real and apparent weakness in the jamb.

All the mouldings of jamb are *invariably sunk from the face of the work.* A projecting mould in such a situation would be a useless excrescence, and contrary to the principles of pointed architecture, which do not admit of any unnecessary members. A hood mould projects immediately above the springing of the arch to receive the water running down the wall over the window, and convey it off on either side. This projection answers a purpose, and therefore is not only allowable but indispensable in the pointed style; but a projection down the sides of jamb, where it would be utterly useless, is never found among the monuments of antiquity.

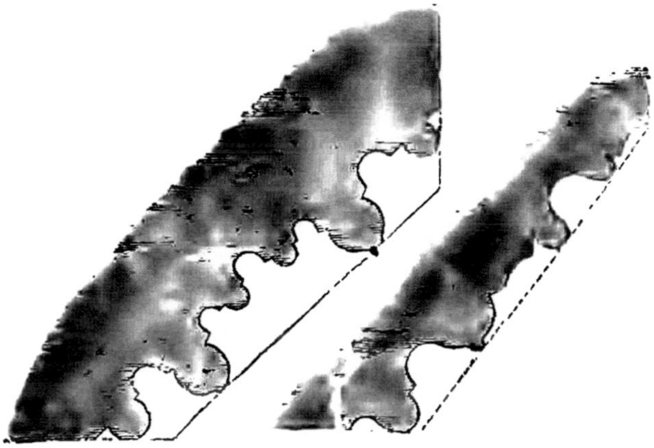

Examples of ancient Jamb Moulds.

Modern Jamb Mould weak and wiry.

French Jamb Mould of the late styles, *extravagantly* hollowed.

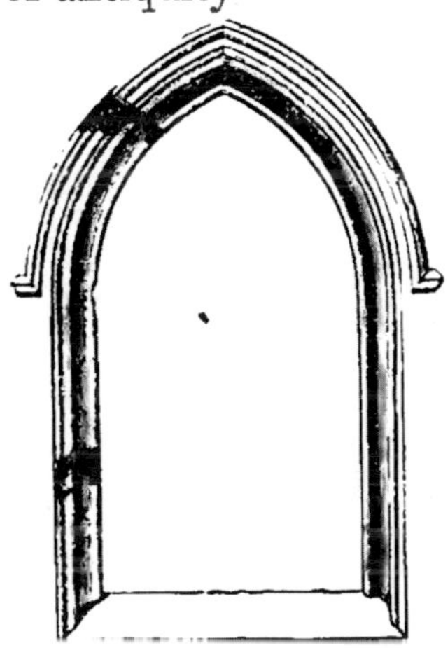

The mouldings round an arch are generally more sub-

Caps at the transition from Jamb to Arch Mould.

divided than those of the jamb. This is carrying out the same principle that may be observed in vegetation, where the solid trunk spreads and divides as it rises upwards. The use of caps at the springing of arches is to receive the different moulds of jamb and arch, which could not be successfully united by any better means than foliated and moulded projections. Hence, in the later pointed continental churches, where the same moulds run up the jambs and round the arches without interruption, caps are entirely omitted; and the same thing is observable, under similar circumstances, in the nave of Crowland Abbey, Lincolnshire.

The next class of mouldings I will notice are those belonging to base

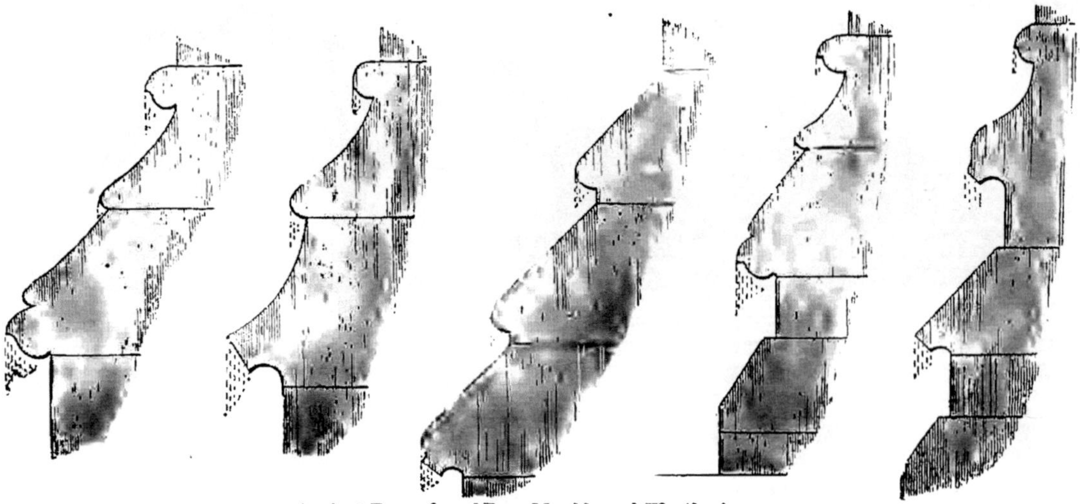

Ancient Examples of Base Moulds and Weatherings.

moulds, weatherings, and strings. I have shewn above that the bevelled form is necessary for these projections; but when the weathering is of any depth, it is evident that the inclined plane cut by the horizontal joints of masonry will produce what are technically called feather-edged joints, at AAA, which would be easily broken by

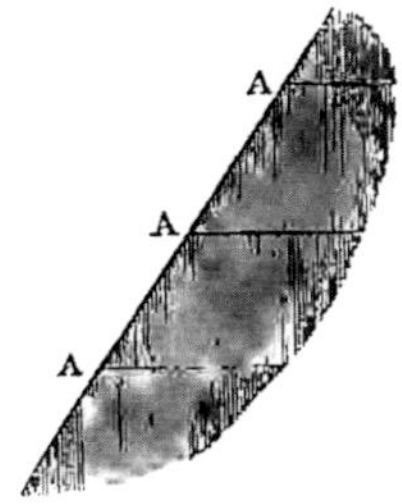

the action of frost, and the joints themselves would be penetrated by water. To obviate this, all the varied and beautiful moulds of weatherings have been introduced, by the form of which the stones are strengthened at the joints, and they are protected from the action of water by the overhanging mould throwing it off to the next bevel.

These observations will apply equally to string-courses and copings.

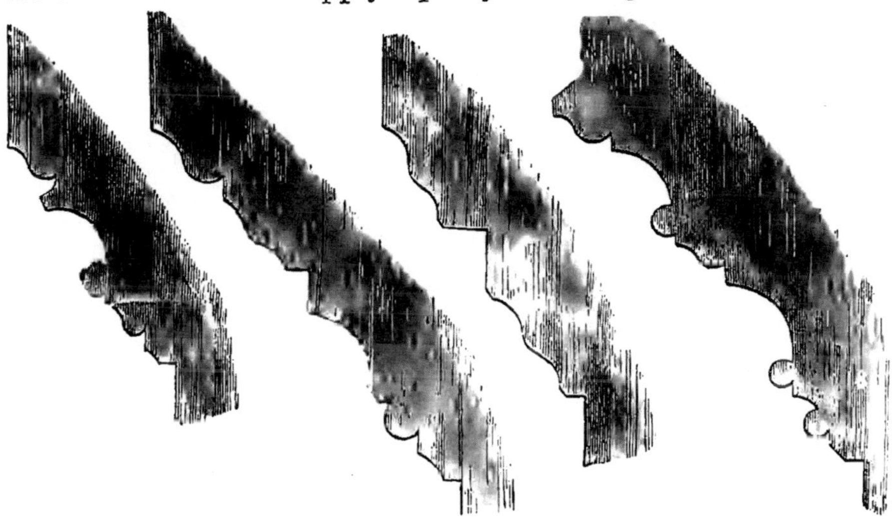

Ancient Profiles of Corbel Moulds.

Another important consideration relative to mouldings, and by which their profile should in a great measure be regulated, is the position in

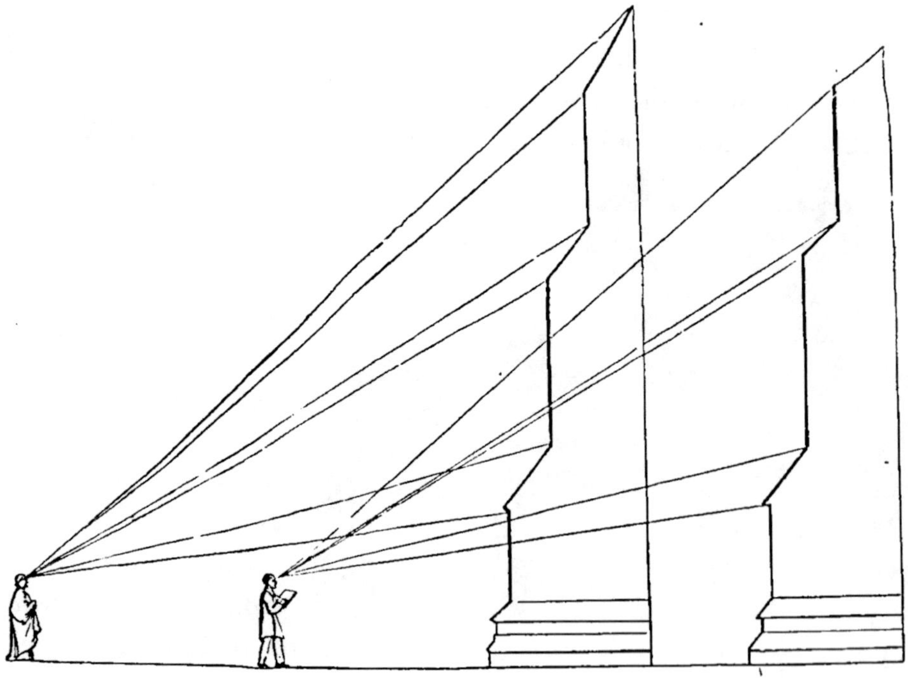

which they are placed with relation to the eye of the spectator. The slope of weatherings themselves is determined by this principle, the pitch increasing with the height that they are placed from the ground. Were this not attended to, the upper water table would be lost to a spectator, unless he was at a considerable distance from the building.

In corbel moulds the profile should *be so formed as to gain projection with strength*, avoiding deep hollows and unnecessary nozings.

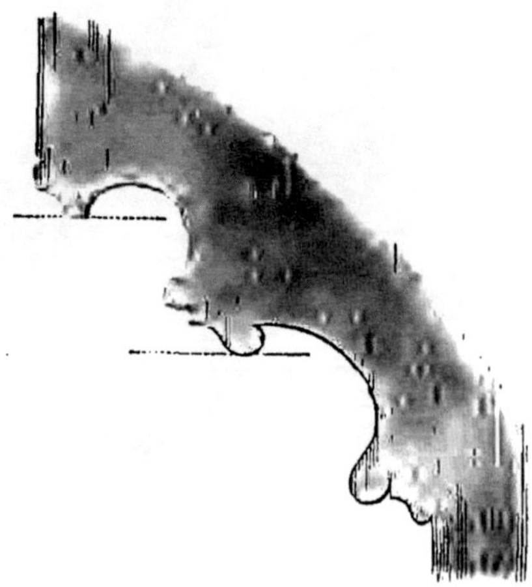

Modern and Weak Corbel Mould.

Fig F

Fig. E

Fig C.

MODERN REGULAR JOINTS

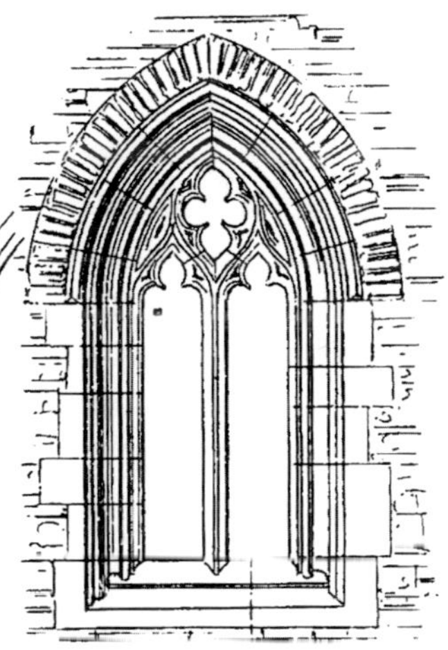

Fig D

ANTIENT IRREGULAR JOINTS

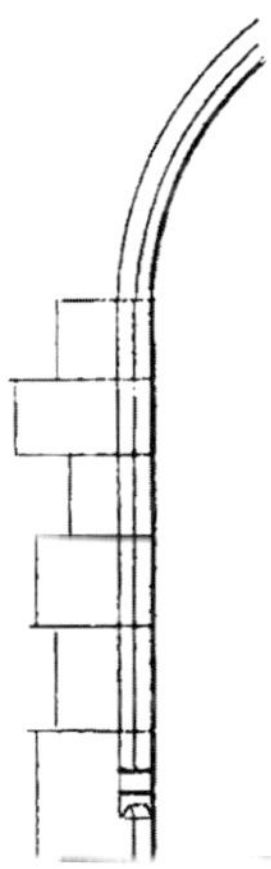

Fig B

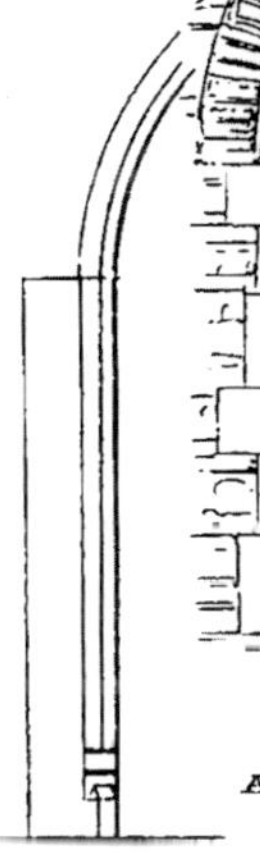

Fig A.

Plate II.

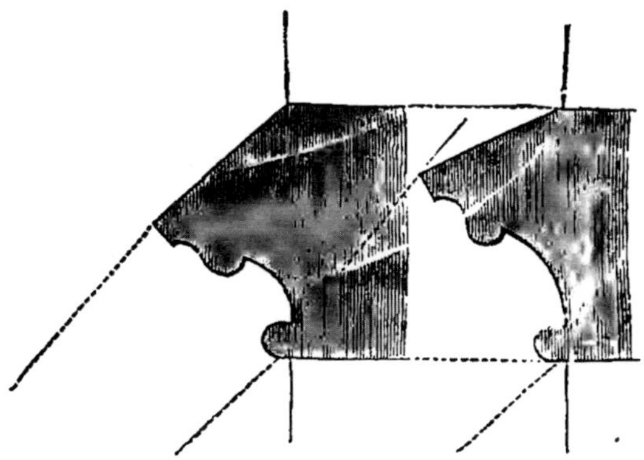

The apparent width of a string-course placed above the eye depends almost as much on the top bevel as on its actual width; for string-courses of equal width, with different bevels, will vary considerably to the eye.

Every moulding in a pointed building must be designed and shaped on these consistent principles. The severity of Christian architecture requires a *reasonable purpose for the introduction of the smallest detail*, and daily experience proves that those who attempt this glorious style without any fixed ideas of its unalterable rules, are certain to end in miserable failures.

Another most important, but now most neglected part of masonry, is the jointing of the stones. All bond and solidity is frequently sacrificed for what is called a neat joint, by setting one stone on end to form a jamb (Plate II. fig. A), when the same space in good old constructions would have been occupied by five or six stones tailing into the wall, and *lying in their natural bed* (fig. B); a point which should be most strictly attended to.

Or, if the jambs are built in courses, they are made as uniform as possible, like rustics (fig. C). By this means the effect of the window is spoiled; the eye, owing to the regularity of these projections, *is carried from the line of jamb to them*, while in the old masonry (fig. D.) the irregular outline of the stones does not interfere with the mouldings of the window.

Another point to be remarked in the ancient masonry is the smallness of the stones employed: now, independently of this being the strongest mode of construction, it adds considerably to the effect of the building by increasing its apparent scale. *Large stones destroy proportion;* and to illustrate this I have given two representations of the same piece of architecture differently jointed. Figs. E, F.

Not only are the stones which are used in the ancient buildings exceedingly small, but they are also very irregular in size, and for the same reason as I have before mentioned, that the jointing might *not appear a regular feature*, and by its *lines interfere* with those of the building.

In the early buildings the work was carried up in regular beds: there were as many joints in a detached pillar as in the wall, and equal space

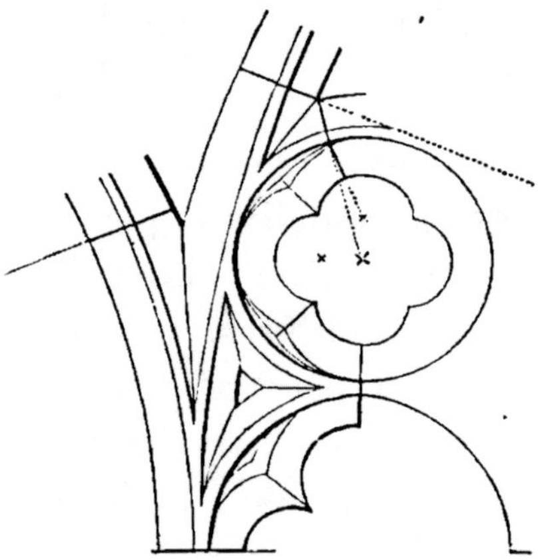

was occupied by the mortar in every part of the building. The joints of stone tracery should always be cut to the centre of the curve where they fall; and if the joint crosses three or four different *curves; its bed should vary with those curves;* and without this is rigidly adhered to in the construction of stone tracery, the work must be devoid of the necessary strength. Any of the great circular or mullioned windows of the ancient cathedrals will fully illustrate this principle.

Images in these northern countries were, with some very few exceptions, placed in niches under canopies. This is really necessary to preserve the sculpture from the injuries of weather, and it is much more consistent than leaving the venerable image of a saintly or royal personage exposed to all the pelting of the pitiless storm. Detached images surmounting buildings, are characteristic of southern and Italian architecture, and are much better suited to the climate of Milan than that of England. (Plate A. fig. 4.)

Having now, I trust, successfully shown that the ornamental parts of pointed stone buildings are merely the decoration of their essential construction, and that the formations of mouldings and details are regulated by practical utility, I will endeavour to illustrate the same principles in ancient metal and wood-work.

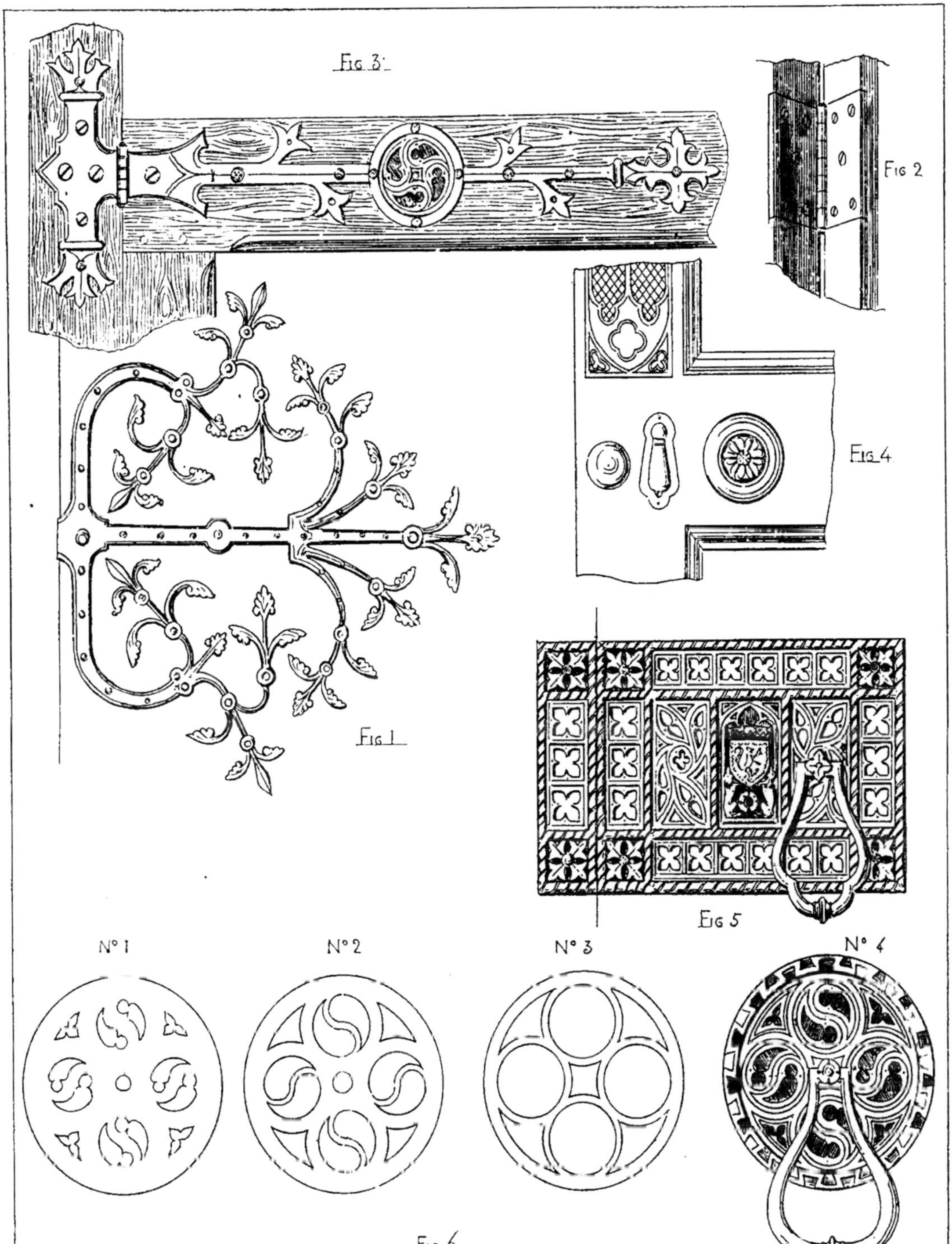

Plate III

ON METAL-WORK.

We now come to the consideration of works in metal; and I shall be able to show that the same principles of suiting the design to the material and decorating construction were strictly adhered to by the artists of the middle ages in all their productions in metal, whether precious or common.

In the first place, hinges, locks, bolts, nails, &c., which are always *concealed in modern designs*, were rendered in pointed architecture, *rich and beautiful decorations;* and this not only in the doors and fittings of buildings, but in cabinets and small articles of furniture.

The early hinges covered the whole face of the doors with varied and flowing scroll-work. Of this description are those of Notre Dame at Paris, St. Elizabeth's church at Marburg, the western doors of Lichfield Cathedral, the Chapter House at York, and hundreds of other churches, both in England and on the continent. Plate III. figs. 1 and 3.

Hinges of this kind are not only beautiful in design, but they are *practically good.* We all know that on the principle of a lever a door may be easily torn off its modern hinges by a strain applied at its outward edge, (fig. 2.) This could not be the case with the ancient hinges, which extended the whole width of the door, and were bolted through in various places. In barn-doors and gates these hinges are still used, although devoid of any elegance of form; but they have been most religiously banished from public edifices as unsightly, merely on account of our present race of artists not exercising the same ingenuity as those of ancient times in rendering the *useful* a vehicle for the beautiful: the same remarks will apply to locks that are now concealed and let into the styles of doors, which are often more than half cut away to receive them. Plate III. fig. 4.

A lock was a subject on which the ancient smiths delighted to exercise the utmost resources of their art. The locks of chests were generally of a most elaborate and beautiful description. A splendid example of an old lock still remains at Beddington Manor House, Surrey, and is engraved in my father's work of Examples. In churches we not unfrequently find locks adorned with sacred subjects chased on them, with the most ingenious mechanical contrivances for concealing the key-hole. Keys were also highly ornamented with appropriate decorations referring to the locks to which they belonged; and even the wards turned into beautiful devices and initial letters. Fig. 5.

In all the ancient ornamental iron-work we may discern a peculiar manner of execution, admirably suited to the material, and quite distinct from that of stone or wood. For instance, tracery was produced by different thicknesses of pierced plates laid over each other. Fig. 6.

Leaves and crockets were not *carved or modelled*, and *then cast*, but cut out of thin metal plate, and twisted up with pliers (Plate IV. figs. 1, 2), and the lines of stems either engraved or soldered on. By these simple means all the lightness, ease, and sharpness of real vegetation is produced at a much less cost than the heavy flat foliage usually cast and chased

Well at Antwerp.

Iron Tracery.

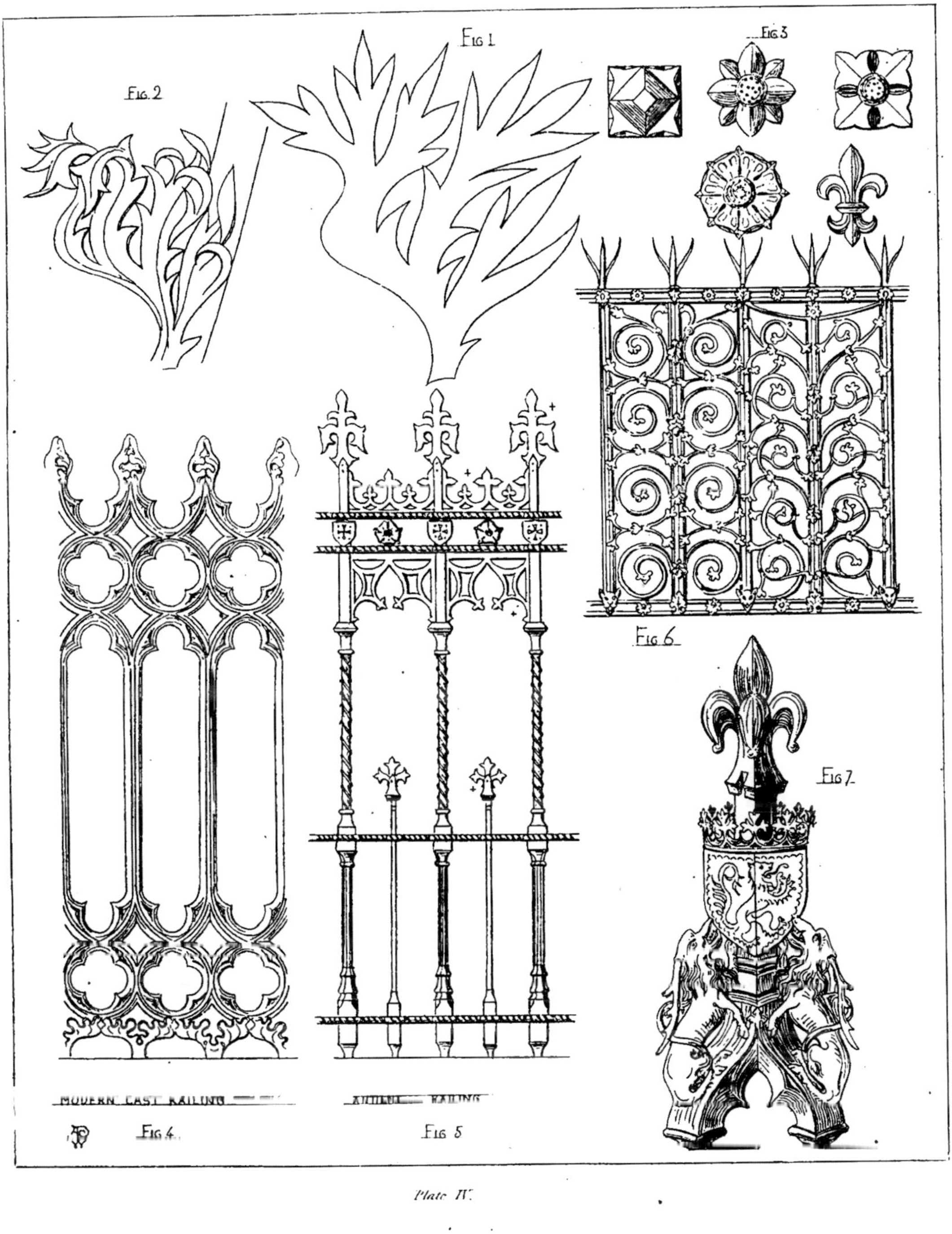
Fig 1
Fig. 2
Fig 3
Fig 6
Fig 7
MODERN CAST RAILING
RAILING
Fig 4.
Fig 5

Plate IV.

Plate B

Fig. I.

Fig II

up. It is likewise to be remarked, that the necessary fastenings for iron-work were always shown and ornamented. Bolts, nails, and rivets, so far from being unsightly, are beautiful studs and busy enrichments, if properly treated. Fig. 3.

Large tracery was either formed of round iron, like a stem twisted into intersections, or of flat iron bars of different thicknesses riveted together, and the edges chamfered by filing.

Railings were not *casts of meagre stone tracery* (Plate IV. fig. 4), but elegant combinations of metal bars, adjusted with due regard to strength and resistance. Fig. 5.*

There were many fine specimens of this style of railing round tombs, and Westminster Abbey was rich in such examples, but they were actually pulled down and sold for old iron by the order of the then Dean, and even the exquisite scroll-work belonging to the tomb of Queen Eleanor, of which I have here given a specimen (fig. 6), was not respected. The iron screen of King Edward the Fourth's tomb at St. George's Chapel, Windsor, is a splendid example of ancient iron-work.

The fire-dogs or Andirons (fig. 7), as they were called, which supported either the fuel-logs where wood was burnt, or grates for coal, were frequently of splendid design. The ornaments were generally heraldic, and it was not unusual to work the finer parts in brass for relief of colour and richness of effect.

These form a striking contrast with the inconsistencies of modern grates, which are not unfrequently made to represent diminutive fronts of castellated or ecclesiastical buildings with turrets, loopholes, windows, and doorways, all in a space of forty inches. (Plate B. fig. 1.)

The fender is a sort of embattled parapet, with a lodge-gate at each end; the end of the poker is a sharp pointed finial; and at the summit of the tongs is a saint. It is impossible to enumerate half the absurdities of

---

* The parts with a + in this figure are merely pierced out of *thin* plate, and riveted to the bars.

modern metal-workers; but all these proceed from the false notion of *disguising* instead of *beautifying* articles of utility. How many objects of ordinary use are rendered monstrous and ridiculous simply because the artist, instead of seeking the *most convenient form*, and *then decorating it*, has embodied some extravagance *to conceal the real purpose for which the article has been made!* If a clock is required, it is not unusual to cast a Roman warrior in a flying chariot, round one of the wheels of which, on close inspection, the hours may be descried; or the whole front of a cathedral church reduced to a few inches in height, with the clock-face occupying the position of a magnificent rose window. Surely the inventor of this patent clock-case could never have reflected that according to the scale on which the edifice was reduced, his clock would be about two hundred feet in circumference, and that such a monster of a dial would crush the proportions of almost any building that could be raised. But this is nothing when compared to what we see continually produced from those inexhaustible mines of bad taste, Birmingham and Sheffield; staircase turrets for inkstands, monumental crosses for light shades, gable ends hung on handles for door-porters, and four doorways and a cluster of pillars to support a French lamp; while a pair of *pinnacles* supporting an arch is called a Gothic-pattern scraper, and a wiry compound of quatrefoils and fan tracery an abbey garden-seat. (Plate B. fig. 2.) Neither relative scale, form, purpose, nor unity of style, is ever considered by those who design these abominations; if they only introduce a quatrefoil or an acute arch, be the outline and style of the article ever so modern and debased, it is at once denominated and sold as Gothic.

While I am on this topic it may not be amiss to mention some other absurdities which may not be out of place, although they do not belong to metal work. I will commence with what are termed Gothic-pattern papers, for hanging walls, where a wretched caricature of a pointed building is repeated from the skirting to the cornice in glorious confusion,—door over pinnacle, and pinnacle over door.

This is a great favourite with hotel and tavern keepers. Again, those papers which are shaded are defective in principle; for, as a paper is hung round a room, the ornament must frequently be shadowed on the light side.

Pattern of Modern Gothic Paper.

The variety of these miserable patterns is quite surprising; and as the expense of cutting a block for a bad figure is equal if not greater than for a good one, there is not the shadow of an excuse for their continual reproduction. A moment's reflection must show the extreme absurdity of *repeating a perspective* over a large surface with some hundred different points of sight: a panel or wall may be enriched and decorated at pleasure, but it should always be treated in a consistent manner.

Flock papers are admirable substitutes for the ancient hangings, but then they must consist of a pattern *without shadow*, with the forms relieved by the introduction of harmonious colours. Illuminated manuscripts of the thirteenth, fourteenth, and fifteenth centuries would furnish an immense number of exquisite designs for this purpose.

These observations will apply to modern carpets, the patterns of which are generally *shaded*. Nothing can be more ridiculous than an apparently *reversed groining* to walk upon, or highly relieved foliage and perforated tracery for the decoration of a floor.

Ancient Pattern for a Flock Paper.

Pattern of Ancient Paving Tiles.

The ancient paving tiles are quite consistent with their purpose, being merely ornamented with a pattern not produced by any apparent relief, but only by *contrast of colour;* and carpets should be treated in precisely the same manner. Turkey carpets, which are by far the handsomest now manufactured, have no shadow in their pattern, but merely an intricate combination of coloured intersections.

Modern upholstery, again, is made a surprising vehicle for bad and paltry taste, especially when any thing very fine is attempted.

To arrange curtains consistently with true taste, their use and intention should always be considered: they are suspended across windows and

MODERN UPHOLSTERY

Fig II.

ANTIENT CURTAIN HANGINGS

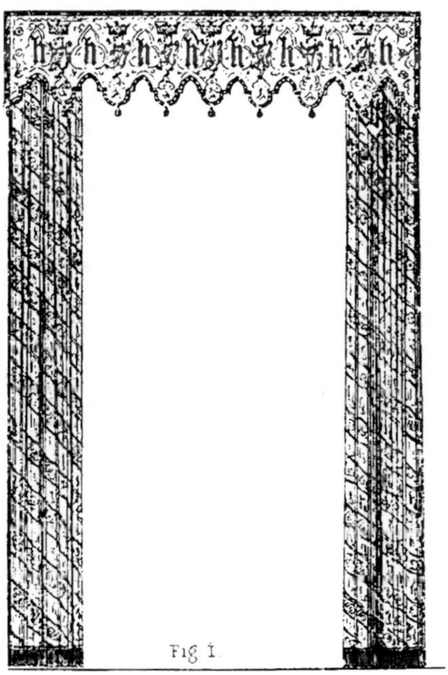

Fig I.

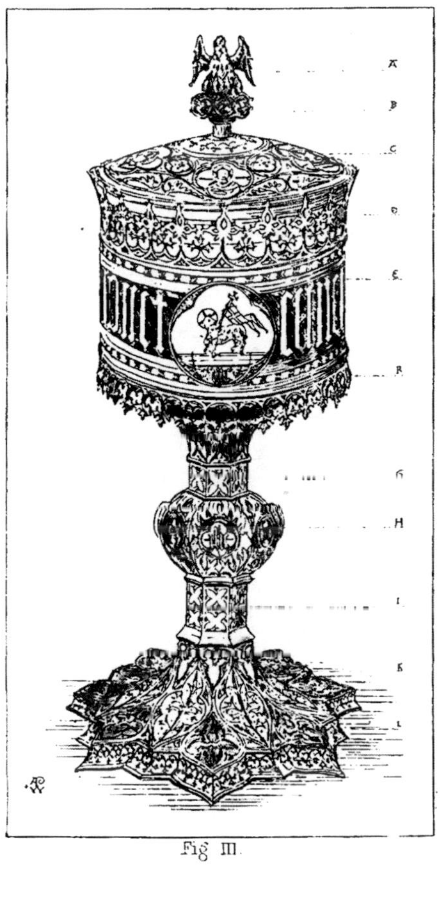

Fig III.

other openings to exclude cold and wind, and as they are not always required to be drawn, they are hung to rings sliding on rods, to be opened or closed at pleasure: as there must necessarily be a space between this rod and the ceiling through which wind will pass, a boxing of wood has been contrived, in front of which a valance is suspended to exclude air.

Now the materials of these curtains may be rich or plain, they may be heavily or lightly fringed, they may be embroidered with heraldic charges or not, according to the locality where they are to be hung, but their real use must be strictly maintained. Hence all the modern plans of suspending enormous folds of stuff over poles, as if for the purpose of sale or of being dried, is quite contrary to the use and intentions of curtains, and abominable in taste; and the only object that these endless festoons and bunchy tassels can answer is to swell the bills and profits of the upholsterers, who are the inventors of these extravagant and ugly draperies, which are not only useless in protecting the chamber from cold, but are the depositories of thick layers of dust, and in London not unfrequently become the strong-holds of vermin. (Plate C, fig. 1.)

It is not less ridiculous to see canopies of tomb and altar screens set up over windows, instead of the appropriate valance or baldaquin of the olden time. It is proper in this place to explain the origin and proper application of fringe, which is but little understood. Fringe was originally nothing more than the ragged edge of the stuff, tied into bunches to prevent it unravelling further. This suggested the idea of manufacturing

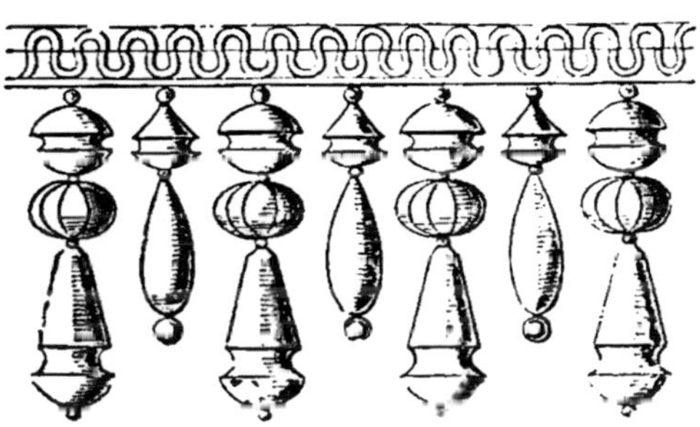

Modern Fringe, composed of turned pieces of wood.

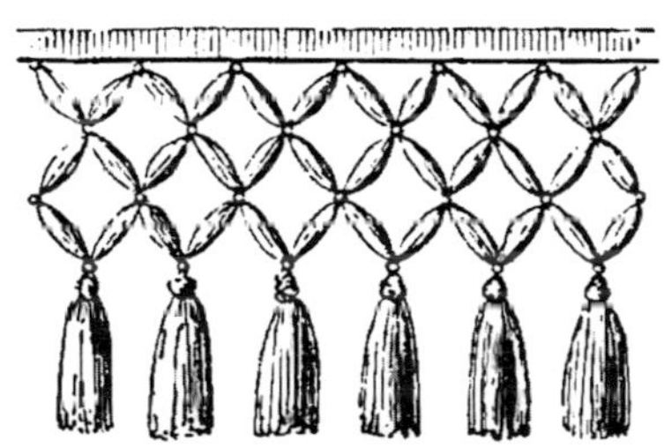

Ancient Fringe, composed of threads.

fringe as an ornamental edging, but good taste requires that it should be both *designed and applied consistently.* (Plate C, fig. 2.)

In the first place, fringe should never consist of *heavy parts*, but simply of threads tied into ornamental patterns.

Secondly, a deep fringe should not be suspended to a narrow valance.

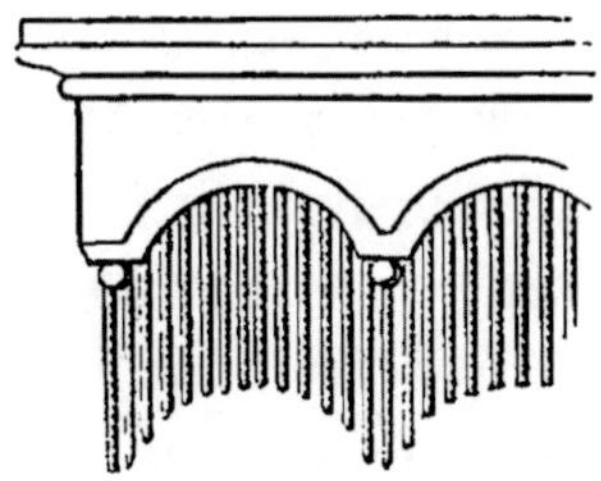

A Modern Valance of Fringe.

Thirdly, no valance should be formed entirely of fringe, as fringe can only be applied as an ornamental edging to some kind of stuff.

Fourthly, fringe should not be sewed *upon* stuff, but always *on the edges.* It is allowable at the very top as it may be supposed to be the upper edge turned over.

But to return to metal-work. We have in the next place to consider the use of cast-iron. When viewed with reference to mechanical purposes, it must be considered as a most valuable invention, but it can but rarely be applied to ornamental purposes.

Iron is so much stronger a material than stone that it requires, of course, a much smaller substance to attain equal strength; hence, to be consistent, the mullions of cast-iron tracery must be so reduced as to look painfully thin, devoid of shadow, and out of all proportion to the openings in which they are fixed. If, to overcome these objections, the castings are made of the same dimensions as stone, a great inconsistency with respect to the material is incurred; and, what will be a much more powerful argument with most people, treble the cost of the usual material.

Cast-iron Mullion.

Stone Mullion.

Moreover, all castings must be deficient of that play of light and shade consequent on bold relief and deep sinkings, so essential to produce a good effect.

Cast-iron is likewise a source of continual repetition, subversive of the variety and imagination exhibited in pointed design. A mould for casting is an expensive thing; once got, it must be worked out. Hence we see the same window in green-house, gate-house, church, and room; the same strawberry-leaf, sometimes perpendicular, sometimes horizontal, sometimes suspended, sometimes on end; although by the principles of pure design these various positions require to be differently treated.

Cast-iron is a deception; it is seldom or never left as iron. It is disguised by paint, either as stone, wood, or marble. This is a mere trick, and the severity of Christian or Pointed Architecture is utterly opposed to all deception: better is it to do a little substantially and consistently with truth than to produce a great but false show. Cheap deceptions of magnificence encourage persons to assume a semblance of decoration far beyond either their means or their station, and it is to this cause we may assign all that mockery of splendour which pervades even the dwellings of the lower classes of society. Glaring, showy, and meretricious ornament was never so much in vogue as at present; it disgraces every branch of our art and manufactures, and the correction of it should be an earnest consideration with every person who desires to see the real principles of art restored.

I will now briefly notice the exquisite productions of the ancient gold and silversmiths. As reformers and puritans have left us nothing but the mere name of the glorious shrine and ornaments which formerly enriched our cathedral and other churches, and as revolutionary and heretical violence has been almost equally destructive on the continent, were it not for a few places which have preserved their ancient treasures, we should be unable to conceive half the art, half the talent, half the exquisite beauties of this class of ecclesiastical ornaments. In the sacristry of Aix-la-Chapelle is a treasury of inestimable value, consisting of shrines, reliquaries, crosses, crowns, ampuls, chalices, pyxes, books of the Holy Gospels, paxes, and enamelled images of silver, all executed during the finest periods of Christian art, the richness of their material being only surpassed by that of their design. To enumerate even a tenth part of these wonderful productions of the goldsmith's art would occupy far too much time for my present purpose; but I will make a few remarks respecting them to illustrate the purpose of my Lecture.

Their construction and execution is decidedly of a *metallic character*. The ornament is produced by *piercing, chasing, engraving, and enamel:* many of the parts were first formed in thin plates of metal, and then shaped by the pliers. Engraving is a style of ornament peculiar to metal. The old goldsmiths were undoubtedly the inventors of our present engraved plates for printing. They increased the effect of the ornamental engravings, by hollowing out the ground in certain parts, and filling it in with coloured enamels. The engraving of an ancient pyx (Plate C. fig. 3.)* will show the style of working silver, as practised during the middle ages. There are some exquisite examples of chalice feet enamelled with sacred subjects in the sacristry of Mayence Cathedral, and a circular reliquary at Aix, which Dr. Rock considers to have been used as a pax, which is a transcendant specimen of the art of enamel. The covers of the great books of the Holy Gospels were enriched with chasing, enamels, and even jewels; the crucifixion of our Lord in the centre, and the emblems of the Evangelists at the corners of an elaborate border. Precious stones of every description were studded on these ornaments, which presented a wonderful combination of richness and beauty, produced by gold enamel of various hues and sparkling gems, arranged with the purest design and most harmonious effect. As it would occupy a whole work to illustrate these objects separately, I have endeavoured to convey some idea of their beauty by the annexed engraving of a reliquary chamber. Plate V.†

---

* References to Plate C. fig. 3.—A. The Pelican, chased. B. The nest, composed of twisted silver wire. C. Engraved and enamelled. D. Pierced and engraved. E. Engraved and the centre enamelled. F. Pierced and engraved. G. Quatrefoils enamelled. H. Knop beat up with enamelled quatrefoils. I. Quatrefoils enamelled. K. Foot hammered up, then engraved and enamelled. L. Engraved.

† References to Plate V.—I. Ferrettum or portable shrine. II., II. Books of the Holy Gospels. III. Relics in a silver bust. IV. Reliquaries. V. Relic of the holy cross.

ALMERY IN A RELIQUARY CHAMBER

Plate V

These treasures, which Aix now alone possesses, were by no means superior to many of those splendid ecclesiastical ornaments formerly to be found in all the large churches of this land, but which fell a prey to the rapacious tyrant Henry and his abettors, in the general wreck of faith and art at the period of his lamentable schism.

Silversmiths are no longer artists; they manufacture fiddle-headed spoons, punchy racing cups, cumbersome tureens and wine-coolers; their vulgar salvers are covered with sprawling rococo, edged with a confused pattern of such universal use that it may be called with propriety the *Sheffield eternal.* Cruet-stand, tea-pot, candlestick, butter-boat, tray, waiter, tea-urn, are all bordered with this in and out shell-and-leaf pattern, which, being struck in a die, does not even possess the merit of relief. Like every thing else, silver-work has sunk to a mere trade, and art is rigidly excluded from its arrangements.

Iron-smiths were artists formerly, and great artists too; Quentin Matsys for instance, whose beautiful well-top stands in front of Antwerp Cathedral, and whose splendid picture of the entombment of our Lord is the greatest ornament of the Musée of that city. Quentin Matsys are not, however, of our generation; if you want some objects executed in iron rather different from what are in ordinary use, and go to a smith to whom you explain your wishes and intentions, the vacant stare of the miserable mechanic soon convinces you that the turning up of a horse-shoe is the extent of his knowledge in the mysteries of the smithy: you then address yourself to another, and one who is called a *capital hand;* and if he be sufficiently sober to comprehend your meaning, he will tell you that what you want is quite out of his line, that he only makes a particular sort of lock, and that he does not think there is a man in the trade who could undertake the job, which, after all, is perhaps a

VI. Paxes for the kiss of peace during the mass. VII. Morse for fastening a cope. VIII. Head of a processional cross. IX. Precious mitres. X. Pastoral staff. XI. Cantor's staff. XII. Images of silver gilt.

mere copy of a very ordinary piece of old iron-work ; and this is a true picture of the majority of our artizans in the nineteenth century, the enlightened age of mechanics' institutes and scientific societies.

Mechanics' institutes are a mere device of the day ; the Church is the true mechanics' institute, the oldest and the best. *She was the great and never failing school in which all the great artists of the days of faith were formed.* Under her guidance they directed the most wonderful efforts of her skill to the glory of God; and let our fervent prayer ever be, that the Church may again, as in days of old, cultivate the talents of her children to the advancement of religion and the welfare of their own souls ;—for without such results talents are vain, and the greatest efforts of art sink to the level of an abomination.

LECTURE II.

WE will now proceed to consider decoration with regard to constructions in wood, which are founded on quite opposite principles to those of stone. With timber you may attain a great height, or extend over a great breadth, by means of a single spar reared on its base or supported at the ends. The strength of wood-work is attained by bracing the various pieces together on geometrical principles. This is beautifully exemplified in ancient roofs, either of churches or domestic buildings : the construction of these, so far from being concealed, is turned into ornament. The principal tie-beams, rafters, purloins, and braces, which in modern edifices are hidden at a vast expense by a flat plaster ceiling, are here rendered very ornamental features, and this essential portion of a building becomes its greatest beauty. Plate VI. figs. 1 and 2.

The stupendous roof of Westminster Hall, decidedly the grandest in the world, illustrates this principle fully, and so do all the roofs in the collegiate halls of Oxford and Cambridge, as well as those of the palatial

ANTIENT ROOF WITH THE FRAMING MADE ORNAMENTAL FIG 1

MODERN ROOF WITH THE FRAMING CONCEALD BY A PLASTERED CEILING FIG 2

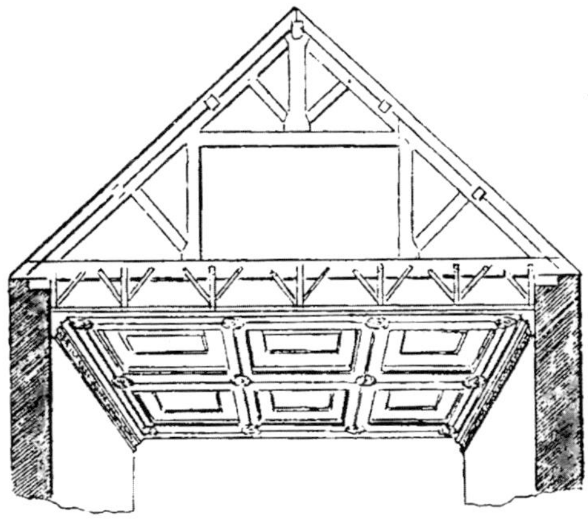

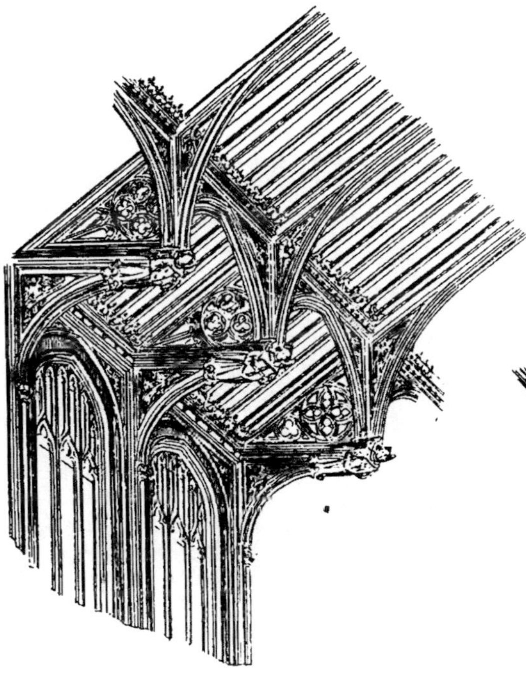

BLAKENEY CHURCH NORFOLK FIG 3

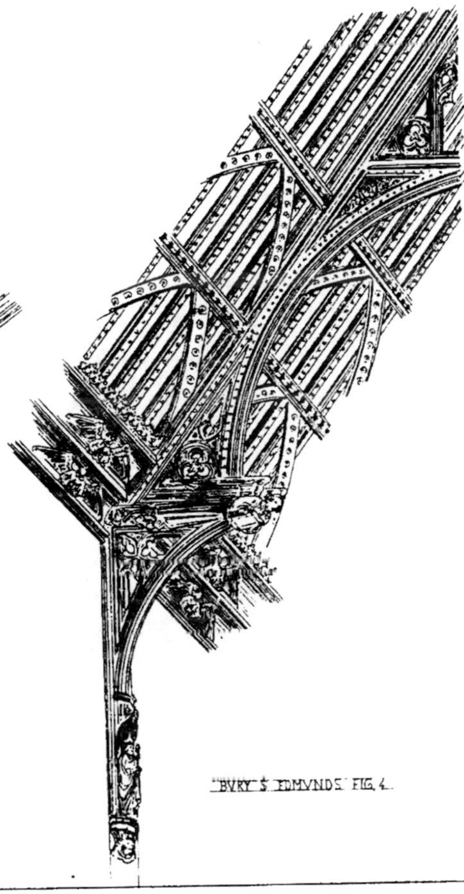

BURY S. EDMUNDS FIG 4

Plate VI

edifices at Eltham, Hampton Court, Croydon, and many others belonging to manorial residences.

Of wooden roofs over churches we have beautiful specimens in various parts of England, but especially in Lincolnshire, Norfolk and Suffolk. The beams of these roofs are beautifully moulded and enriched with carvings. Figs. 3, 4.

Nor were these carvings without a mystical and appropriate meaning; they usually represented angels, archangels, and various orders of the heavenly hierarchy, hovering over the congregated faithful, while the spaces between the rafters were painted azure and powdered with stars and other celestial emblems, a beautiful figure of the firmament. Some of these angels held shields charged with the instruments of the passion, the holy name, and other emblems; others labels with devout scriptures. Every portion of these roofs was enriched with painting, and when in their glory must have formed splendid canopies to the temples of the living God; and what is peculiarly useful to illustrate my present purpose, these roofs were of an entirely different construction to coverings of stone. *Wooden groining* is decidedly bad, because it is employing a material *in the place and after the manner of stone, which requires an entirely different mode of construction.*

I am aware that ancient examples of wooden groining are to be found in the cloisters of Lincoln Cathedral, Selby Church, and some others; but in these cases, as well as any others in which it may be found, an inspection of the building will clearly show that they were originally intended to have been groined with stone, and that the springing ribs have been carried up some height in that material, but that owing to a real or supposed weakness in the side walls, which were not considered capable of resisting the lateral pressure of stone vaulting, the expedient of an imitation groining in wood was resorted to as a case of absolute necessity; and I am decidedly of opinion that had not the original intention been to have groined these churches in stone, their builders would have made an entirely different arrangement in their upper parts, suitable to an ornamental wooden roof.

At Bury St. Edmund's is a glorious roof, of which I have given a sketch. At every pair of principals are two angels as large as the human figure, bearing the sacred vessels and ornaments used in the celebration of the holy sacrifice; these angels are vested in chasubles and dalmaticks, tunicles and copes, of ancient and beautiful form; the candlesticks, thurible, chalice, books, cruets, &c., which they bear are most valuable authorities for the form and design of those used in our ancient churches. The roofs of St. Peter's and All Saints, in that truly catholic city of Norwich, are very fine; and in Lavenham and Long Melford churches, in Suffolk, are admirable specimens of carved timber roofs.*

But, alas! how many equally fine roofs have been demolished and burnt by the brutal ignorance of parish functionaries!—how many have been daubed over by the remorseless whitewasher!—how many painted in vile imitation of marble, as at Yarmouth, (especially if the churchwarden for the time being happened to be a *grainer!*)—how many of these fine roofs have been spoiled of their beautiful and appropriate decorations by the execrable fanaticism of the puritan faction, who actually have made entries in the parish accounts of the cost of their demolition!—how many concealed from view by lath and plaster ceilings of miserable design tacked up under them!—and although a somewhat better spirit has at length arisen, still how many of these beautiful memorials of the piety and skill of our ancestors are yet being mutilated or utterly destroyed under the pretext of reparation!—a plea which is not unfrequently urged by those in authority for selling the lead and massive oak beams, the solid covering of antiquity, and substituting a plastered ceiling and meagre slates in their stead, which detestable practice is still in full force in many parts of England. (Plate D, fig. 1.)

Not only do we find the construction of roofs ornamented, but there

* In a past number of the British Critic is a most admirable article on open roofs, well worthy the perusal of all who are interested in the revival of ancient ecclesiastical architecture.

Plate D.

Fig. II

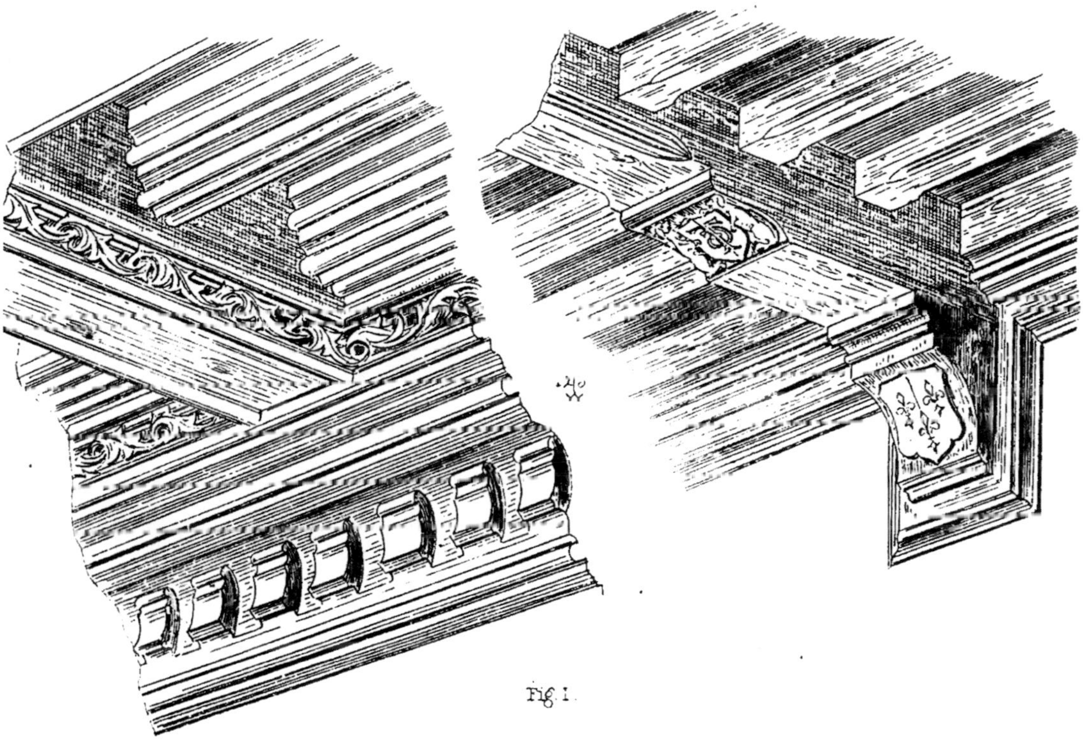

Fig. I.

Plate. E.

are numerous examples of common joist floors and the carrying beams which are rendered exceedingly beautiful by moulding and carving.* (Plate D. fig. 2.)

In the ancient timbered houses of which such interesting examples yet remain in many of our old cities, especially at Coventry, York, and Gloucester, we do not *find a single feature introduced beyond the decoration of what was necessary for their substantial construction.* What can be stronger, and at the same time more ornamental, than the curvilineal bracing by which due advantage was taken of crooked pieces of timber!—The ancient French cities, Rouen, Beauvais, Abbeville, Liseux, and others, were full of timber houses covered with carved beams and most varied ornaments; (Plate E.) but these are rapidly disappearing to make way for monotonous plaster buildings, which are constructed also of *wood;* but as modern architects have not the skill to ornament that construction, the whole of the timbers are *concealed by mock cornices and pilasters*, so that the houses of modern Rouen have all the disadvantages of the old wooden buildings, without one particle of their beauty.

As gable-ends form most prominent features of the old buildings, and as they are continually attempted by modern Gothic builders, I will draw your attention to their real use, and then point out some of the egregious blunders frequently committed by modern architects when they attempt to introduce them.

The barge boards of gables are intended to cover and preserve the ends of the purloins which projected over to shelter the front of the building.

The hip knop which terminated the ancient gables was in reality a king post fixed at the junction of the barge boards, and into which they were tenanted. To the upper part of these was usually affixed

* The ground of the ceiling of the Clopton Chauntry, Long Melford is azure: the stars are of lead, gilt; the inscription on the rafters is Jhū Mercy, and Gramercy; the arms on the shields are those belonging to different branches of the Clopton family, with their names inscribed beneath. The scripture on the large scroll is extracted from the Psalter, the whole richly painted.

a vane, and the bottom was finished off in the form of a pendant. Plate VII.

In modern gable ends the barge boards are generally so *slight and cut so open* that they become mere skeletons, and utterly useless for the purpose for which they should be fixed, that of covering the timber ends. Again, the knop really useful at the apex of the gable is repeated in modern gables at the extremities, hanging down to an extravagant depth, and loaded with bunchy finials and pendants. Pl. VII.

Of these we may say with Puff in the Critic, when he hears the three morning guns, "Give these fellows a good idea, and they will work it to death." A king post in the centre of the gable is good, because it is really useful, but at the lower extremities these excrescences cannot serve any purpose except to add useless weight and unnecessary expense.

It is a common practice, when a chimney shaft is carried up in the centre of a gable end, for the barge boards *to be fixed before it.* This is absurd; flues must necessarily stop the passage of timbers; consequently the barge boards, which are only coverings of those timbers, should stop also. Pl. VII.

If we examine the ancient wood-work which decorated rooms, we shall find that it consisted of mere panelling more or less enriched by carving, with large spaces left for hangings and tapestry. Plate VIII.

Were the real principles of Gothic architecture restored, the present objection of its extreme costliness would cease to exist. In pointed decoration *too much* is generally attempted; every room in what is called a Gothic house must be fitted with niches, pinnacles, groining, tracery, and tabernacle work, after the manner of a chantry or chapel. Such fittings must be enormously expensive, and

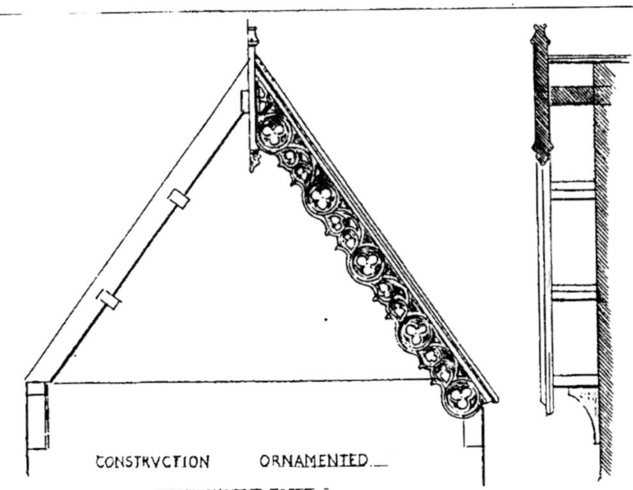

CONSTRUCTION ORNAMENTED

IN AN ANCIENT GABLE

GABLE IN THE VILLA GOTHIC STYLE

GABLE IN FRONT OF A CHIMNEY

Plate VII

Plate VIII.

Plate F

at the same time they are contrary to the true spirit of the style, which does not admit of the introduction of these features in any situation but that to which they properly belong. The modern admirers of the pointed style have done much injury to its revival by the erroneous and costly system they have pursued: the interiors of their houses are one mass of elaborate work; there is no repose, no solidity, no space left for hangings or simple panels: the whole is covered with trifling details, enormously expensive, and at the same time subversive of good effect. These observations apply equally to furniture;—upholsterers seem to think that nothing can be Gothic unless it is found in some church. Hence your modern man designs a sofa or occasional table from details culled out of Britton's Cathedrals, and all the ordinary articles of furniture, which require to be simple and convenient, are made not only very expensive but very uneasy. We find diminutive flying buttresses about an arm-chair; every thing is crocketed with angular projections, innumerable mitres, sharp ornaments, and turreted extremities. (Plate F.) A man who remains any length of time in a modern Gothic room, and escapes without being wounded by some of its minutiæ, may consider himself extremely fortunate. There are often as many pinnacles and gablets about a pier-glass frame as are to be found in an ordinary church, and not unfrequently the whole canopy of a tomb has been transferred for the purpose, as at Strawberry Hill. I have perpetrated many of these enormities in the furniture I designed some years ago for Windsor Castle. At that time I had not the least idea of the principles I am now explaining; all my knowledge of Pointed Architecture was confined to a tolerably good notion of details in the abstract; but these I employed with so little judgment or propriety, that, although the parts were correct and exceedingly well executed, collectively they appeared a complete burlesque of pointed design.

I now come, in the last place, to consider decoration with reference to propriety; what I mean by propriety is this, *that the external and internal appearance of an edifice should be illustrative of, and in accordance with, the purpose for which it is destined.* There is a vast difference between a building raised to God and one for temporal purposes; again, in the first of these a great distinction necessarily exists between a cathedral and a parochial church, between a collegiate chapel and a private oratory; and in the second, between a royal residence, and a manorial mansion,—between monuments raised for public or national purposes and erections for private convenience.

The scale of propriety in architecture must always be regulated by purpose, and to illustrate this more fully I will divide edifices under three heads,—Ecclesiastical, Collegiate, and Civil. The greatest privilege possessed by man is to be allowed, while on earth, to contribute to the glory of God: a man who builds a church draws down a blessing on himself both for this life and that of the world to come, and likewise imparts under God the means of every blessing to his fellow creatures; hence we cannot feel surprised at the vast number of religious buildings erected by our Catholic forefathers in the days of faith, or at their endeavours to render those structures, by their arrangement and decoration, as suitable as their means could accomplish for their holy and important destination. It must have been an edifying sight to have overlooked some ancient city raised when religion formed a leading impulse in the mind of man, and when the honour and worship of the Author of all good was considered of greater importance than the achievement of the most lucrative commercial speculation. There stood the mother church, the great cathedral, vast in height, rising above all the towers of the parochial churches which surrounded her; next in scale and grandeur might have been discerned the abbatial and collegiate churches with their vast and solemn buildings; each street had its temple raised for the true worship of God, *variously beautiful in design, but each a fine example of Christian art.* Even the bridges and approaches were not destitute of religious buildings, and many a beautiful chapel and oratory was corbelled out in massive piers over the stream that flowed beneath.

The great object I have in directing your attention to such a Catholic city is to illustrate the principle of decorative propriety in ecclesiastical buildings. We have here various edifices of various dimensions, various degrees of richness, various in arrangement, yet each bears on its very face the stamp of Catholic;—cathedral or abbey, church or oratory, they all show that they are dedicated to the one true faith, raised by men actuated by one great motive, the truly Catholic principle of dedicating the best they possessed to God. It would be both unjust and unreasonable to expect a few parishioners to erect as sumptuous an edifice to the Almighty as the clergy of a vast cathedral, and even if they could practically achieve such a result, it would be out of character for the use and intentions of a parish church; neither ought we to look to a private chapel or oratory erected by the unassisted piety of an individual for the extent or ornaments of a public church, unless, indeed, that individual was possessed of great wealth, and then, although not in dimensions, it should surpass in glory the usual decoration of such buildings. In a word architectural propriety as regards ecclesiastical buildings requires that they should be as good, as spacious, as rich and beautiful, as the *means and numbers of those who are erecting them will permit.* The history of our present vast and magnificent churches fully exemplifies this principle; many of them in their origin were little better than thatched barns; it was the best that could be done at that early period: but when the wealth and influence of the church increased, they were soon demolished to make way for more fitting structures; these in their turn were rebuilt with still greater magnificence. The ancient clergy were never satisfied, never content, never imagined that they had done enough; the scaffoldings were round the walls and the cranes on the towers of many of the English abbeys at the time of their suppression.

It is not incumbent on all men to raise vast and splendid churches; but it *is* incumbent on all men to render the buildings they raise for religious purposes *more vast and beautiful than those in which they dwell.* This is all I contend for; but this is a feeling nearly if not altogether extinct. Churches are now built without the least regard to tradition, to mystical reasons, or even common propriety. A room full of seats at the least possible cost is the present idea of a church; and if any ornament is indulged in, it is a mere screen to catch the eye of the passer-by, which is a most contemptible deception to hide the meanness of the real building. How often do we see a front gable carried up to a respectable pitch, and we might naturally infer that this is the termination, both as regards height and form, of the actual roof; but on turning the corner we soon perceive that it is a mere wall cramped to hold it in its position, and that it conceals a very meeting-house, with a flat roof and low thin walls, perforated by mean apertures, and without a single feature or detail to carry out the appearance it assumes towards the street. (Plate G. fig. 1.) Now the severity of Christian architecture is opposed to all deception. We should never make a building erected to God appear better than it really is by artificial means. These are showy worldly expedients, adapted only for those who live by splendid deception, such as theatricals, mountebanks, quacks, and the like. Nothing can be more execrable than making a church appear rich and beautiful in the eyes of men, but full of trick and falsehood, which cannot escape the all-searching eye of God, to whom churches should be built, and not to man. Even under the Mosaic dispensation, the Holy of Holies, *entered only by the high priest*, was overlaid with gold; and how much more ought the interiors of our tabernacles to be lined with precious material, which are ten times more holy and deserving of it than the figurative tabernacle of the old law!—and yet in these times all that does not *catch the eye is neglected.* A rich looking antipendum often conceals rough materials, a depository for candle ends, and an accumulation of dirt, which are allowed to remain simply because they are out of sight. All plaster, cast-iron, and composition ornaments, painted like stone or oak, are mere impositions, and, although very suitable to a tea-garden, are utterly unworthy of a sacred edifice. "Omne secundum ordinem et honeste fiat." Let every man build to God according to his means, but not practise showy deceptions; better is it to do a little substantially and consistently with truth, than to

Plate 6

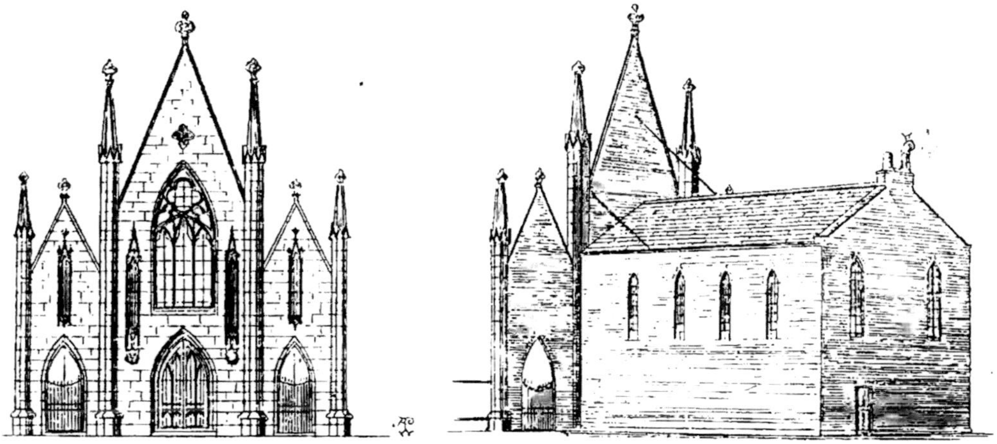

Fig. I

Fig. II.

Fig. III.

produce a great but fictitious effect. Hence the rubble wall and oaken rafter of antiquity yet impress the mind with feelings of reverent awe, which never could be produced by the cement and plaster imitations of elaborate tracery and florid designs which in these times are stuck about mimic churches in disgusting profusion.

It is likewise essential to ecclesiastical propriety that the ornaments introduced about churches should be appropriate and significant, and not consist of *Pagan* emblems and attributes for buildings professedly erected for Christian worship. If the admirers of *classic* decoration were consistent, on the very principles which induced the ancients to set up their divinities, they should now employ other and more appropriate ornaments; as all those found in the temples and other buildings of the Pagans were in strict accordance with their mythology and customs; *they never introduced any emblem without a mystical signification being attached to it.* It would be unjust to charge the advocates of revived Pagan decoration with an actual belief in the mythology of which they are such jealous admirers; hence they are guilty of the greater inconsistency, as the original heathens proceeded from conviction. They would not have placed urns on the tombs, had they not practised burning instead of burying their dead; of which former custom the urn was a fitting emblem, as being the depository for the ashes. Neither would they have decorated the friezes with the heads of sheep and oxen, had they not sacrificed those animals to their supposed gods, or placed inverted torches on the mausoleums, had they believed in the glories of the Resurrection. But what have we as *Christians*, to do with all those things illustrative *only of former error?* Is our wisdom set forth by the owl of Minerva, or our strength by the club of Hercules? What have we (who have been redeemed by the sacrifice of our Lord himself) to do with the carcasses of bulls and goats? And how can we (who surround the biers of our departed brethren with blazing tapers, denoting our hope and faith in the glorious light of the Resurrection,) carve the *inverted torch of Pagan despair* on the very tomb to which

Modern Tomb in the revived Pagan style.

we conduet their remains with sueh sparkling light? Let us away with sueh gross ineonsisteneies, and restore the Christian ideas of our Catholie aneestors, for they alone are proper for our imitation. But not only are the details of modern ehurches borrowed from Pagan instead of Christian antiquity, but the very plan and arrangement of the buildings themselves are now fashioned after a heathen temple; for which unsightly and inappropriate form modern ehurehmen and architeets have abandoned those whieh are not only illustrative of the great mysteries of the Christian faith, but whose use has been sanetioned by the eustom of more than twelve eenturies.

I will now give the following distinet reasons why the arehiteeture of the Greek temples eannot be introdueed or imitated with propriety by Christians.

1. These temples were ereeted for an idolatrous worship, and were suited only for the idolatrous rites whieh were performed in them.

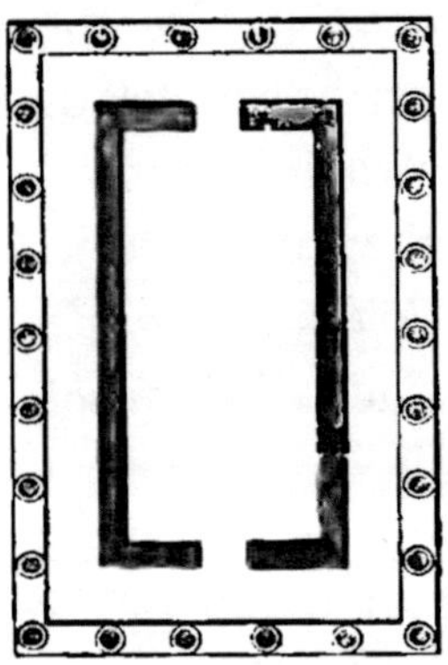

The interior, entered only by the priests, was eomparatively small, and either dark or open at the top, while the peristyle and portieoes were spaeious, for the people who assisted without. There is not the slightest similarity between our worship and the idolatrous worship of the Greeks. We require that the people should be *within* the ehureh, not outside. If, therefore, you adopt a perfeet Greek temple, your interior will be eonfined and ill-suited for the intended purpose, while your exterior will oeeasion an enormous outlay without any utility. If, on the other hand, you strip a Greek temple of its external peristyle, and build your external walls in the place of the pillars, you entirely destroy the most beautiful feature of the architecture, and the building becomes a miserable departure from the style it professes to imitate.

2. The Greeks did not introduce windows in their temples; they are essentially necessary with us. Perforate the walls with windows, and you again destroy the simplicity and unity of Greek architecture, which its admirers extol as one of its greatest beauties.

3. Christian churches require bells, by the sound of which the faithful may be called to their devotions. The bells to be distinctly heard, must be suspended in a tower or belfry, and these are features utterly unknown in Greek architecture. A tower composed of a number of small porticoes, set over one another, and placed in front of a mock temple, is a most glaring absurdity; nor is a tower of this description, starting out of nothing at the top of a portico, any better. (Plate G. figs. 2 and 3.)

4. Our northern climate requires an acute pitch of roof to prevent the accumulation of snow and to resist weather.[5] The Greeks, whose climate is the reverse of ours, had their roofs and pediments exceedingly flat; nor could they be raised to our proper pitch without violating the character of their architecture. Fig. 3.

Fig. 3.

In short, Greek temples are utterly inapplicable to the purpose of Christian churches;[6] and the attempt is little short

[5] It is to be remarked that flat-pitched roofs were not introduced into English pointed churches till after the decline of that style, and the marks of the old high gabled roofs are generally to be seen in the towers of those churches where the present roofs are flat, proving them to have been altered subsequent to the original erection of the buildings.

[6] Neither are they better adapted for domestic purposes; for it is still more absurd to see two or three tiers of windows introduced in the shell of a Greek temple, the roof of

of madness when our country is literally covered with beautiful models of ecclesiastical structures of every dimension, *the architecture and arrangement of which have originated in their wants and purpose.* An old English parish church, as originally used for the ancient worship, was one of the most beautiful and appropriate buildings that the mind of man could conceive; every portion of it answered both a useful and mystical purpose. There stood the tower, not formed of *detached and misapplied* portions of architectural detail stuck over one another to make up a height, but solid buttresses and walls rising from a massive base, and gradually diminishing and enriching as they rise, till they were terminated in a heaven-pointing spire surrounded by clusters of pinnacles, and forming a beautiful and instructive emblem of a Christian's brightest hopes. These towers served a double purpose, for in them hung the solemn sounding bells to summon the people to the offices of the church, and by their lofty elevation they served as beacons to direct their footsteps to the sacred spot. Then the southern porch, destined for the performance of many rites,—the spacious nave and aisles for the faithful,—the oaken canopy carved with images of the heavenly host, and painted with quaint and appropriate devices,—the impressive doom or judgment pictured over the great chancel arch,—the fretted screen and rood loft,—the mystical separation between the sacrifice and the people, with the emblem of redemption carried on high and surrounded with glory,—the great altar, rich in hangings, placed far from irreverent gaze, and with the brilliant eastern window terminating this long perspective; while the chantry and guild chapels, pious foundations of families and confraternities, contributed greatly to increase the solemnity of the glorious pile. (Plate H. fig. 1.) Such is

---

which is broken by numerous stacks of vainly disguised chimneys. Yet notwithstanding the palpable impracticability of adapting the Greek temples to our climate, habits, and religion, we see the attempt and failure continually made and repeated: post-office, theatre, church, bath, reading-room, hotel, methodist chapel, and turnpike-gate, all present the eternal sameness of a Grecian temple outraged in all its proportions and character. (Plate H. fig. 2.)

Plate II.

Fig. I.

Fig. II.

Fig. III.

but a faint outline of the national edifices which have been abandoned for pewed and galleried assembly rooms, decorated only with gas fittings and stoves, and without so much as one holy or soul-stirring emblem about them.

We will now examine architectural propriety with reference to collegiate architecture. Our old English Catholic colleges (Plate IX.) will illustrate most beautifully the principle I wish to demonstrate. The main feature of these buildings was the chapel: to our Catholic forefathers the celebration of the divine office with becoming solemnity and splendour formed a primary consideration, and ample was the provision made for this purpose in all the old collegiate foundations. The place set apart for this holy purpose generally towered over the surrounding buildings. The chapels of Kings College and Eton can be distinctly seen many miles before the subordinate buildings can be discerned. Oxford, at a distance, presents a complete grove of towers, spires, and pinnacled turrets, rising from the collegiate churches. After this principal feature, every portion of these edifices had its distinguishing character and elevation; in order to give due effect to the gate-house, refectory, and other important parts of the building, the chambers never exceeded the height of one story above the ground floor.[7] A very characteristic feature of the old collegiate buildings is the position of the chimneys, which are made to project from the front walls of the buildings. This, I am well aware, has been considered a defect by ignorant modern artists, but will be found on examination, like all other practices of the ancient architects, to be based on excellent practical reasons.

The advantages of this arrangement are as follow: 1. All the internal

[7] In those ancient colleges where these chambers have been raised in modern times, the effect of the original design has been completely ruined, and the new collegiate buildings at St. John's, Cambridge, from their height have all the appearance of a Gothic warehouse or factory. This is another instance of the folly of using pointed details without following the spirit of the ancient buildings

space usually occupied by chimney stacks, and which is very considerable, is gained to the apartments.—2. The stacks of chimneys thus placed act as buttresses to the wall.—3. The danger of fire consequent upon chimney flues passing through the wood-work of the roofs is entirely avoided.—4. A great variety of light and shadow, and a succession of bold features, are gained in the building. (Plate H. fig. 3.) It is impossible to conceive any buildings better adapted for collegiate purposes, either as regards arrangement or design, than the two establishments founded by that great and good man, William of Wykeham, at Winchester and Oxford. He had two classes to consider in his foundation at Winchester, the clergy and the students. For the former he provided beautiful cloisters retired from the rest of the edifice, suited for contemplation and devotion; while for the latter he assigned ample space for healthy recreation in bad weather, and level meadows for summer sports. The whole character of these buildings is at once severe, elegant, and scholastic; it is precisely what it should be, as the will of Henry the Sixth specifies of the domestic portion of his college at Cambridge, that it should be built *without too great superfluity of detail or busie moulding*;[s] and on this principle Wykeham designed his building. The external ornaments are few, but admirably selected: an image of our blessed Ladye with our Lord is placed over each gateway, in reference to the college being dedicated to God, under the invocation of his blessed mother, towards whom the good bishop entertained an extraordinary devotion, even from his tender years. The other images

---

[s] Notwithstanding the directions contained in this will, where the founder's intentions regarding his collegiate buildings are fully and distinctly expressed, the architect (when the glorious opportunity offered a few years since of fulfilling them to the letter, and erecting a truly fine building) was allowed to depart entirely from them, and raise a florid structure, arranged in direct opposition to all old collegiate traditions, and the very decorations of which were misapplied details taken from the original chapel, which had been elaborately enriched by the ancient builders for the purpose of distinguishing its sacred destination from the surrounding erections.

on either side of the centre niche are those of the angel Gabriel, and Wykeham himself in a kneeling position.

The interior of the chapel (now woefully disfigured) as left by the founder, must have been glorious in the extreme; it consisted of a choir and ante-chapel, by the side of which rose the bell tower, simple, but elegant and lofty.

The members of the society were buried in the cloisters, and also in the ante-chapel, as their memorials of beautifully engraved brass testify. The intention of these was, doubtless, both to incite the surviving community to pray for their souls' repose, and to remind them continually of the similar fate that would inevitably befall them. How Catholic wisdom and Catholic piety stand conspicuous in all the arrangements of these noble buildings! how great the master mind who planned and executed them, and yet how few are there in these days able to understand or willing to imitate them! Can we conceive a more atrocious scheme to destroy the solemn grandeur of Wykeham's church than to allow such a man as Sir Joshua Reynolds to design a transparency for the western end, and appoint *James Wyatt the destructive* to overturn the ancient features and arrangements, setting up the subsellæ of the stalls as brackets for book-desks, and covering the walls with meagre decorations and Bernasconi Gothic!

Modern collegiate buildings,[9] especially on the continent, are the reverse of all that I have been describing. In them we look in vain for the solemn quadrangle, the studious cloister, the turreted gate-house, the noble refectory with its oak-beamed roof, the mullioned windows and pinnacled parapet, and lofty tower of the church: not a ghost of these venerable characteristics of a college is to be seen, but generally one

[9] It is impossible to conceive a more uncollegiate looking building than what is called the London University, with its useless dome and portico. It may, however, be urged in its defence that any thing *ecclesiastical or Christian* would be very inappropriate, and that the *Pagan* exterior is much more in character with the intentions and principles of the institution.

uniform mass, unbroken either in outline or in face, undistinguishable from other large buildings which surround it. As to its purpose, it might

be taken for a barrack hospital or asylum. How is it possible to expect that the race of men who proceed from these factories of learning will possess the same feelings as those who anciently went forth from the Catholic structures of Oxford and Winchester! We cannot sufficiently admire our English universities; there is nothing like them existing on the continent, notwithstanding the miserable additions and modernizations which have so greatly disfigured the ancient buildings. There is more Catholic scholastic architecture to be found united at Oxford than in any place I have ever visited. Let us hope and pray that its glories may not exist in vain, but that learned and thinking men may be led to draw a parallel in their minds between the faith of those good souls who founded these noble institutions, and our present degraded and half-infidel condition, by which consideration they may be led back to Catholic unity and faith, in which great works can be alone accomplished, or blessings derived from them.

In the third and last place, we will consider architectural propriety with reference to domestic and civil architecture. Most of the mansions erected at the present day in the Italian or pointed architecture, are either burlesques or false application of both these styles. In the first place, what does an Italian house do in England? Is there any similarity between our climate and that of Italy? Not the least. Now I will maintain and prove that climate has always had a large share in the formation of domestic architecture, and the Italian is a good illustration of the truth of this remark. The apertures are small; long colonnades for shade, and the whole building calculated for retreat, and protection from heat; the roofs are flat in pitch, from the absence of heavy snow; and plan and outline are both suited to the climate to which the architecture belongs. But

Plate. 1

Fig II

Fig I.

we demand in England the very reverse of all this for comfort. We cannot fortunately import the climate of a country with its architecture, or else we should have the strangest possible combination of temperature and weather; and, within the narrow compass of the Regent's Park, the burning heat of Hindoostan, the freezing temperature of a Swiss mountain, the intolerable warmth of an Italian summer, with occasional spots of our native temperature. (Plate I. fig. 1.) I wonder if these ideas ever occur to those who design Italian gardens on the moorlands of England. Truly it will not be a matter of surprise if some searcher after novelty try to cultivate a jungle for imitation tiger-hunting on some old English estate.

Another objection to Italian architecture is this,—we are not Italians we are Englishmen. God in his wisdom has implanted a love of nation and country in every man, and we should always cultivate the feeling:—we ought to view the habits and manners of other nations without prejudice, derive improvement from all we observe admirable, but we should never forget our own land. Such is, indeed, the extraordinary amalgamation of architecture, style, and manners now in progress, that were it not for the works of nature which cannot be destroyed, and the glorious works of Christian antiquity which have *not yet* been destroyed, Europe would soon present such sameness as to cease to be interesting. Already a sort of bastard Greek, a nondescript modern style, has ravaged many of the most interesting cities of Europe; replacing the original national buildings with unmeaning lines of plaster fronts, without form, without colour, without interest. How many glorious churches have been destroyed within the last few years (*pour faire une place*) for the occasional exercise of the national guard! where a few stunted trees and a puddle of water in a stone basin, which spouts up occasionally some few feet in height, is all we have to see in exchange for some of the most interesting memorials of ancient piety.

England is rapidly losing its venerable garb; all places are becoming alike; every good old gabled inn is turned into an ugly hotel with a stuccoed portico, and a vulgar coffee-room lined with staring paper, with imitation scagliola columns, composition glass frames, an obsequious cheat of a waiter, and twenty per cent. added to the bill on the score of the modern and elegant arrangements. Our good old St. Martin's, St. John's, St. Peter's, and St. Mary's streets, are becoming Belle-vue Places, Adelaide Rows, Apollo Terraces, Regent Squares, and Royal Circuses. Factory chimneys disfigure our most beautiful vales; Government preaching-houses, called Churches, start up at the cost of a few hundreds each, by the side of Zion chapels, Bethel Meetings, New Connections, and Socialist Halls. (Plate I. fig. 2.) Timbered fronts of curious and ingenious design are swept away before the resistless torrent of Roman-cement men, who buy their ornaments by the yard, and their capitals by the ton. Every linen-draper's shop apes to be something after the palace of the Cæsars; the mock stone columns are fixed over a front of plate glass to exhibit the astonishing bargains; while low-ticketed goods are hung out over the trophies of war. (Plate K. fig. 1.) But this is not all; every paltry town has a cigar divan, with something stuck out to look Turkish, and not unfrequently a back parlour travestied into a vile burlesque of eastern architecture. In short, national feelings and national architecture are at so low an ebb, that it becomes an absolute duty in every Englishman to attempt their revival. Our ancient architecture can alone furnish us with the means of doing this successfully; but unfortunately, those who profess to admire pointed architecture, and who strive to imitate it, produce more ridiculous results than those who fly to foreign aid. What can be more absurd than houses built in what is termed the castellated style? Castellated architecture originated in the wants consequent on a certain state of society: of course the necessity of great strength, and the means of defence suited to the military tactics of the day, dictated to the builders of ancient castles the most appropriate style for their construction. Viewed as historical monuments, they are of surprising interest, but as models for our imitation they are worse than useless. What absurdities, what anomalies, what utter contradictions do not the builders of modern castles perpetrate! How many portcullises which will not lower down, and drawbridges which will not

Plate. K.

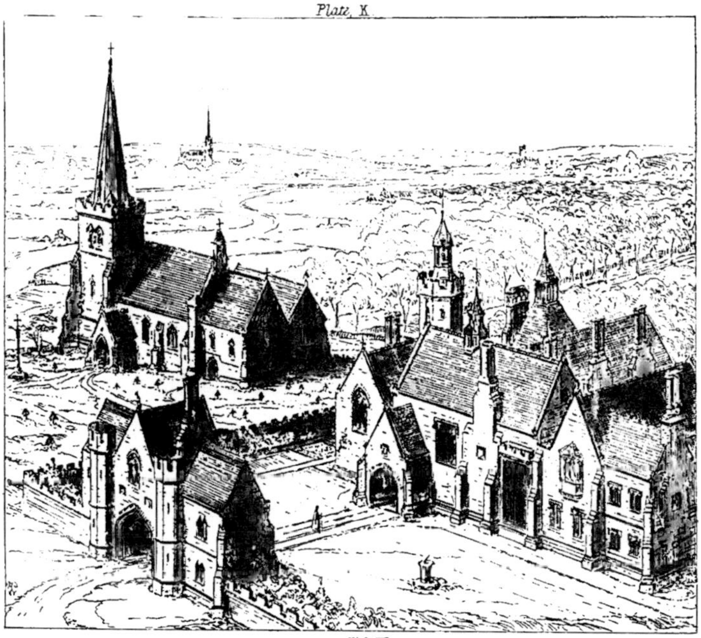

Fig III.

Fig I

Plate. K.

Fig II.

draw up !—how many loop-holes in turrets so small that the most diminutive sweep could not ascend them !—On one side of the house machicolated parapets, embrasures, bastions, and all the show of strong defence, and round the corner of the building a conservatory leading to the principal rooms, through which a whole company of horsemen might penetrate at one smash into the very heart of the mansion !—for who would hammer against nailed portals when he could kick his way through the greenhouse? In buildings of this sort, so far from the turrets being erected for any particular purpose, it is difficult to assign any destination to them after they are erected, and those which are not made into *chimneys* seldom get other occupants than the rooks. But the exterior is not the least inconsistent portion of the edifice, for we find guard-rooms without either weapons or guards; sally-ports, out of which nobody passes but the servants, and where a military man never did go out; donjon keeps which are nothing but drawing-rooms, boudoirs, and elegant apartments; watch-towers, where the house-maids sleep, and a bastion in which the butler cleans his plate: all is a mere mask, and the whole building an ill-conceived lie. (Plate K. fig. 2.)

We will now turn to those mansions erected in what is termed the Abbey style, which are not more consistent than the buildings I have just described. To this class Fonthill belonged, now a heap of ruins, and modern ruins, too, of mere brick and plaster. In such a house something of an ecclesiastical exterior had been obtained at an enormous expense, and a casual passer-by might have supposed from some distance that the place really belonged to some religious community; but on a nearer approach the illusion is soon dissipated, and the building, which had been raised somewhat in the guise of the solemn architecture of religion and antiquity, discovers itself to be a mere toy, built to suit the caprice of a wealthy individual, and devoted to luxury. The seemingly abbey-gate turns out a modern hall, with liveried footmen in lieu of a conventual porter; the apparent church nave is only a vestibule; the tower, a lantern staircase; the transepts are drawing-rooms; the cloisters, a furnished passage ; the oratory, a lady's boudoir ; the chapter-house, a dining-room ; *the kitchens alone* are real ; every thing else is a deeeption. Articles of fashionable luxury, glasses in profusion, couehes and ottomans, fill the ehambers of the moek eonvent, from whenee a prayer never ascends or into whieh a religious man never enters ;—all, in fine, is a moekery and thing of fashion, transient and perishable as the life of its possessor ; and if the strueture be substantial enough to last his time, it soon after beeomes the subjeet of some auetioneer's puff : its walls are eovered with plaeards ; brokers divide the moveables ; the whole falls to decay, and is soon only mentioned as a splendid folly.

The old English Catholie mansions were the very reverse of those I have been deseribing ; they were substantial appropriate edifiees, suited by their scale and arrangement for the purposes of habitation. Each part of these buildings indieated its partieular destination : the turreted gate-house and porter's lodging, the entranee poreh, the high-crested roof and Louvred hall, with its eapaeious chimney, the guest ehambers, the vast kitchens and offiees, all formed distinet and beautiful features, not *masked or concealed under one monotonous front*, but by their variety in form and outline inereasing the effeet of the building, and presenting a standing illustration of good old English hospitality ; while the venerable parish chureh in the immediate vicinity, with its grey spire and family chantry, showed that the eare spiritual was not negleeted by our aneestors in the ereetion of their temporal dwellings. (Plate K. fig. 3.)

Every person should be lodged as beeomes his station and dignity, for in this there is nothing eontrary to, but in aeeordanee with, the Catholie prineiple ; but the mansions ereeted by our aneestors were not the passing whim of a moment, or mere show plaees raised at such an extravagant eost as impoverished some generations of heirs to the estates, but solid, dignified, and Christian struetures, built with due regard to the general prosperity of the family ; and the almost constant residenee of the aneient gentry on their estates rendered it indispensable for them to have mansions where they might exercise the rights of hospitality to their fullest extent. They did not confine their guests, as at present, to a few fashionables who condescend to pass away a few days occasionally in a country house; but under the oaken rafters of their capacious halls the lords of the manor used to assemble all their friends and tenants at those successive periods when the church bids all her children rejoice, while humbler guests partook of their share of bounty dealt to them by the hand of the almoner beneath the groined entrance of the gate-house. Catholic England was merry England, at least for the humbler classes; and the architecture was in keeping with the faith and manners of the times,—at once strong and hospitable. There is a great reviving taste for ancient domestic architecture, but a vast many pretended admirers of old English beauties, instead of imitating the Tudor period, when domestic architecture was carried to a high state of perfection, stop short at the reign of Elizabeth, the very worst kind of English architecture; and, strange to say, these unmeaning conglomerations of debased forms have been classed into a regular style, and called after the female tyrant during whose reign they were executed. The only reason I can assign for the fashionable rage for this architecture (if so it may be called) is, that its character is so corrupt, mixed, and bad, that the anachronisms and anomalies so frequently perpetrated by modern architects are made to pass muster under the general term of Elizabethan; and certainly I cannot deny that the appellation is very appropriate when applied to corrupted design and decayed taste.

I must here mention two great defects very common in modern pointed buildings, both of which arise from the great fundamental principle of decorating utility not being understood. In the first place, many architects apply the details and minor features of the pointed style to classic *masses* and arrangements; they adhere scrupulously to the regularity and symmetry of the latter, while they attempt to disguise it by the mouldings and accessories of the former. They must have two of every thing, one on each side: no matter if all the required accommodation is contained in one half of the design, a shell of another half must be built to keep up uniformity. What can be more absurd? Because a man has a real door to enter his house by on one side, he must have a mock one through which he cannot get in on the other. How inconsistent is it to make and glaze a window which is to be *walled up* ab initio! But to see the full absurdity of this system, let us only imagine the builders of the ancient colleges, after having finished a church and refectory on one side of a quadrangle, running up something to repeat them by way of a pendant on the other, so as to appear two churches and two dining-halls to one college. In the second place, when modern architects avoid this defect of regularity, they frequently fall into one equally great with regard to irregularity; I mean when a building is *designed to be picturesque*, by sticking as many ins and outs, ups and downs, about it as possible. *The picturesque effect of the ancient buildings results from the ingenious methods by which the old builders overcame local and constructive difficulties.* An edifice which is arranged with the principal view of looking picturesque is sure to resemble an artificial waterfall or a made-up rock, which are generally so *unnaturally natural* as to appear ridiculous.

An architect should exhibit his skill by turning the difficulties which occur in raising an elevation from *a convenient plan* into so many *picturesque beauties;* and this constitutes the great difference between the principles of classic and pointed domestic architecture. In the former *he would be compelled to devise expedients to conceal these irregularities;* in the latter *he has only to beautify them.* But I am quite assured that all the irregularities that are so beautiful in ancient architecture are the result of certain necessary difficulties, and were never purposely designed; for to make a building inconvenient for the sake of obtaining irregularity would be scarcely less ridiculous than preparing working drawings for a new ruin. But all these inconsistencies have arisen from this great error, —*the plans of buildings are designed to suit the elevation, instead of the elevation being made subservient to the plan.*

Plate L.

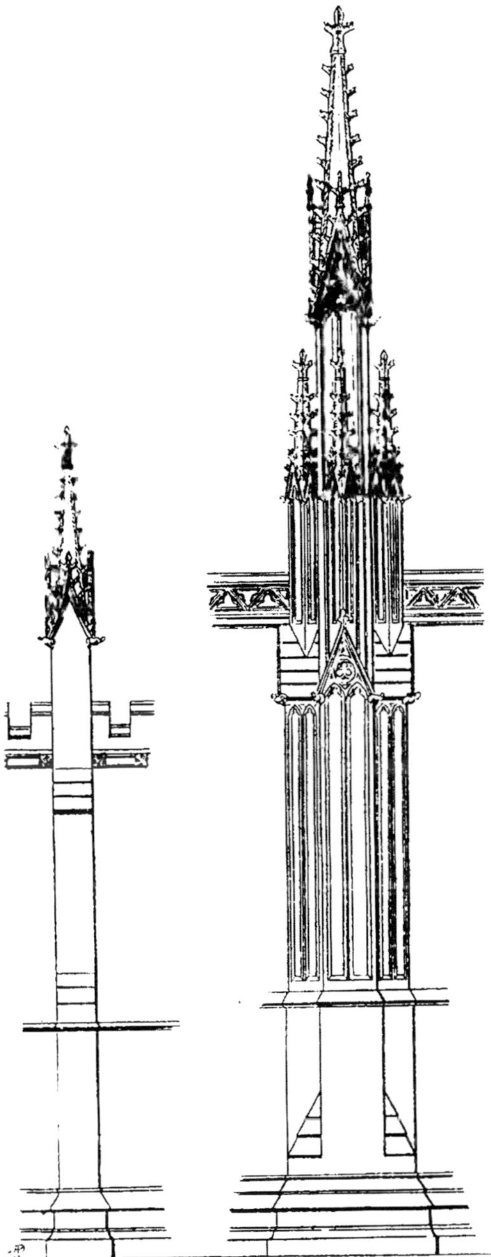

Fig. 1.

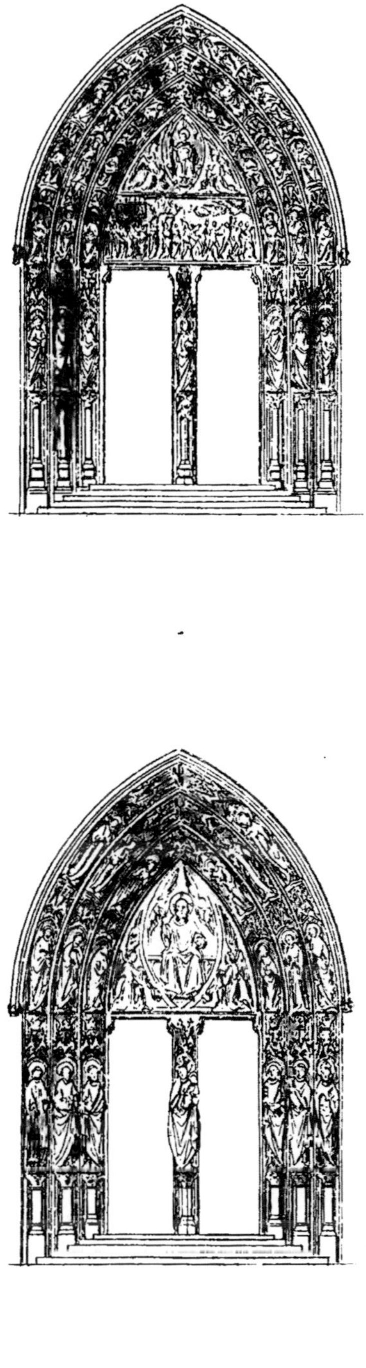

Fig II

Under the head of architectural propriety we have also to consider the scale and proportions of buildings. Without vastness of dimensions it is impossible to produce a grand and imposing effect in architecture; still, unless these be regulated on true principles, they may destroy their effect by their very size; and here I wish to draw your attention to a point which will prove the great superiority of the Christian architecture of the middle ages over that of classic antiquity, or of the revived pagan style. In pointed architecture the different details of the edifice are *multiplied with the increased scale of the building:* in classic architecture they are *only magnified.*

To explain this more fully, if the pointed architects had a buttress and pinnacle to erect against some vast structure, such as the Cathedral of Cologne or Amiens, they did not merely increase its dimensions by gigantic water tables, enormous crockets, and a ponderous finial. No! they subdivided it into a *cluster* of piers and pinnacles; they panelled the front, enriched it by subordinate divisions, and by these means the pinnacles of Cologne appear five times as large as those of an ordinary church,[10] which could never have been the case had they only *enlarged the scale instead of multiplying the parts.* (Plate L, fig. 1.) But the very reverse of this is the case in classic architecture; a column or cornice is the same, *great or small,* whether they are employed in front of an ordinary house or of a vast temple; no distinction except that of size is ever made; there are the *same number of diameters,* the *same number of mouldings,* the *same relative projections;*—it is merely a *magnifying power* applied to architecture. What is the result? Till you

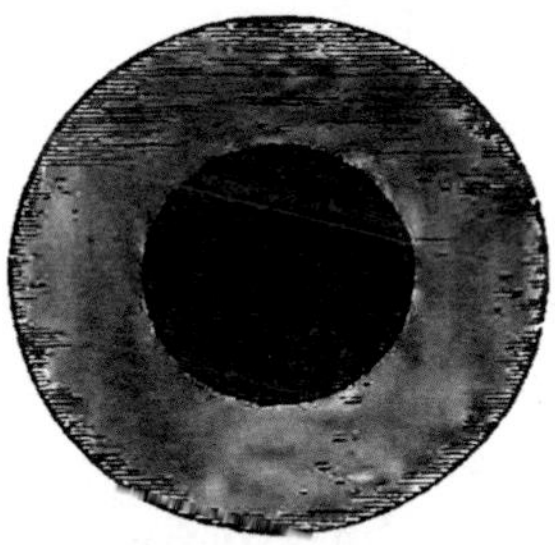

[10] A pillar in classic architecture is a mere cylinder, of large or small diameter. In the pointed style a pillar is subdivided into shafts, which increase in number with its size, and form beautiful clusters.

actually stand under these buildings, and find that your chin does not come up to the plinth at the base, you do not perceive the scale. This is perfectly exemplified at St. Peter's. The effect on all who first enter it is that of disappointment; it does not appear any thing like so large as they anticipated. Some of its admirers have tried to pass this off as a great beauty, and have attributed it to its beautiful proportion. This reasoning will not, however, stand the test of close examination; it is essentially false. One of the great arts of architecture is to render a building more vast and lofty in appearance than it is in reality. The contrary effect produced by St. Peter's is not the least among its many defects, and it is purely owing to the *magnifying* instead of the *multiplying principle* having been followed. The great size of its various parts and mouldings required the introduction of colossal figures, which are certain to reduce the appearance of size in any buildings where they are used.

The human figure is a general standard for scale. We are accustomed to assimilate the idea of about five feet nine inches with the height of a man. Hence, be a drawing ever so small, by inserting a diminutive human figure it will immediately convey an idea of the intended size; and on the contrary, if the figures in a drawing be over large, the apparent space represented is immediately reduced in appearance. So is it in architecture: a figure of eighteen feet high will reduce one hundred feet to less than forty in appearance; and the mystery of the disappointing effect of scale in St. Peter's is satisfactorily accounted for. It is all very well for guides and valets de place to astonish travellers by stating that three persons may sit on the great toe of a statue, or that if a figure were laid on its back five men might straddle across the nose; *so much the worse for the effect of the building where such a figure is placed.*

In pointed architecture we seldom find any images larger than the human size, and generally much less. Hence the surprising effect of height and scale conveyed by many old Catholic buildings, which are not in reality half the size of some of their more modern and semi-pagan rivals at Rome. (Plate L, fig. 2.)

In general our English churches are deficient in internal height; not that our national style of Christian art does not possess some fine specimens of this important feature, as in the glorious church of St. Peter, Westminster; but I think the internal vastness of Amiens, Beauvais, Chartres, and others of the French churches, should serve as useful examples to us in this respect in the revival of Pointed and Christian architecture in England. Nothing can be conceived more majestic than those successions of arches divided by light and elegant clusters of shafts running up to an amazing height, and then branching over into beautiful intersected ribs, suspending a canópy of stone at the enormous height of not unfrequently one hundred and fifty feet. Internal altitude is a feature which would add greatly to the effect of many of our fine English churches, and I shall ever advocate its introduction, as it is a characteristic of foreign pointed architecture of which we can avail ourselves without violating the principles of our own peculiar style of English Christian architecture, from which I would not depart in this country on any account. I once stood on the very edge of a precipice in this respect, from which I was rescued by the advice and arguments of my respected and reverend friend Dr. Rock, to whose learned researches and observations on Christian antiquities I am highly indebted, and to whom I feel it a bounden duty to make this public acknowledgment of the great benefit I have received from his advice. Captivated by the beauties of foreign pointed architecture, I was on the verge of departing from the severity of our English style, and engrafting portions of foreign detail and arrangement. This I feel convinced would have been a failure; for although the great principles of Christian architecture were every where the same, each country had some peculiar manner of developing them, and we should continue working in the same parallel lines, all contributing to the grand whole of Catholic art, but by the very variety increasing its beauties and its interest.

In conclusion, Christian verity compels me to acknowledge that there are hardly any defects which I have pointed out to you in the course of this Lecture which could not with propriety be illustrated by my own productions at some period of my professional career. Truth is only gradually developed in the mind, and is the result of long experience and deep investigation. Having, as I conceive, discovered the true principles of pointed architecture, I am anxious to explain to others the errors and misconceptions into which I have fallen, that they, profiting by my experience, may henceforward strive to revive the glorious works of Christian art in all the ancient and *consistent* principles. Let then the Beautiful and the True be our watchword for future exertions in the overthrow of modern paltry taste and paganism, and the revival of Catholic art and dignity.

+

Laus Deo!